by Emlyn Williams

SAMUELFRENCH-LONDON.CO.UK
SAMUELFRENCH.COM

EMLYN WILLIAMS
Playwright

Emlyn Williams, 'the Welsh Noël Coward', was one of the most popular writers of the 1930s and 1940s. Born George Emlyn WIlliams, he was raised in a Welsh-speaking, working class family in Flintshire, Wales. Williams (1905-1987) combined a dazzling commercial instinct with daring, edgy writing that pushed the boundaries of acceptable theatre.

From the time of his definitive success in 1935 in his own play *Night Must Fall*, Emlyn Williams was an outstanding figure in the British and American theatre as actor, playwright and director. His other plays include *The Light of Heart, Spring 1600, The Wind of Heaven, Someone Waiting, Trespass* and *The Corn Is Green*, in which he starred with Sybil Thorndike at the Duchess Theatre. The American production starred Ethel Barrymore and the play was filmed with Bette Davis and - later - Katherine Hepburn. He also worked with Alfred Hitchcock and Carol Reed as a screenwriter. Productions of his work starred Ethel Barrymore and Gregory Peck, and more recently Ian McKellen, Deborah Kerr, Mathew Broderick and Jason Donovan. Williams' numerous stage appearances in London and New York included *The Winslow Boy* (Rattigan) and *Montserrat* (Hellman), while his appearances in films include *The Citadel, The Stars Look Down, Major Barbara, Hatter's Castle, Ivanhoe* and *The Last Days of Dolwyn* (which he also directed, having written it for Edith Evans and Richard Burton) and an historical curiosity, the unfinished *I, Claudius*.

Williams often acted in his own plays (he played Will Trenting in *Accolade*), and was famous for his one-man-shows, with which he toured the world, playing Charles Dickens in an evening of excerpts from Dickens' novels. This "one man show" was the start of a whole new theatrical genre. He was also the "voice" of Lloyd-George in the seminal BBC documentary *The Great War* (1964) and narrated the investiture of Charles as Prince of Wales in 1969.

His autobiography in two volumes – *George: An Early Autobiography* (1961) and *Emlyn* (1973) – was highly successful. In it, he wrote frankly of his bisexuality and his early homosexual experiences. He married in 1935 and had two sons: Alan, a writer, and Brook, an actor. His wife, Molly Shann, died in 1970. A lifelong bisexual who came 'out' ahead of most of his contemporaries, Williams balanced his marriage and family life with a series of flings. The stresses of leading a double life are explored in *Accolade*.

Williams was appointed a Commander of the Order of the British Empire in 1962, and was an honorary LL.D of the University of Wales. He died in Chelsea on September 25 1987, aged 81.

ACCOLADE

Emlyn Williams was fascinated by abnormal psychology both as an actor and dramatist. As a writer he created out-of-the-ordinary characters and as an actor he brought them to life. ACCOLADE was based on his firm belief that we all have something to be ashamed of, as a dual personality exists in each of us.

His creation of Will Trenting, a married, successful novelist whose sexual attraction to disreputable people provides material for his books, wins our sympathy despite the sinister revelations. In fact this reflected Williams' personal life, as his wife and family knew of his own two lives. Emlyn Williams' autobiographies "George" and "Emlyn" were dedicated to his wife Molly and sons Alan and Brook, and were explicit about his bisexuality.

Emlyn worked on ACCOLADE for the best part of a year during his appearance in New York in MONTSERRAT, writing a scene and revising it after a lapse of time had permitted the draft to "go cold". The play took longer to write than any of his previous works, as it had to be constructed with infinite care in order to sustain the suspense of the story and avoid what audiences might find offensive in Trenting's character. The play proved to be one of the most moving and provocative of the 1950s, having surprisingly been approved by the censor (the Lord Chamberlain) who did not require the deletion of a single word.

I spent my theatregoing years in the 1940s and 1950s in admiration of the versatility of such creative talents as Noel Coward and Emlyn Williams. Noel Coward's range as a writer extended to such works as BITTER SWEET, CAVALCADE, BRIEF ENCOUNTER and DESIGN FOR LIVING. It is indeed timely that the first revival of ACCOLADE since its premiere in 1950 at the Finborough Theatre in 2011 should follow on from the revival of DESIGN FOR LIVING, in which (in 1932) Coward explored the eroticism of a "ménage-a-trois". Both these plays were much more outspoken about homosexuality than the hidden aspects in Terence Rattigan's THE DEEP BLUE SEA and SEPARATE TABLES. In 1946 Emlyn Williams had appeared in Rattigan's THE WINSLOW BOY with tremendous success.

There are many plays by Emlyn Williams worthy of revival, but the great interest in ACCOLADE is that the dramatist gives the audience no clue as to how the trial will turn out. Always a master of suspense, Williams leaves each playgoer to have the satisfaction of rounding off the story to his own liking. Williams pointed out that the important issue is not Trenting's sentence or acquittal but the fact that he has learnt how difficult it is for successful people to survive media attention. What could be more topical now, over half a century later?

Anthony Field (1928–2014)
www.anthonyfieldassociates.com

Accolade was first presented in London by H. M. Tennent Ltd, in association with Leland Hayward and Joshua Logan, at the Aldwych Theatre, on September 7 1950, with the following cast:

Will Trenting	**Emlyn Williams**
Albert	**Anthony Oliver**
Rona	**Diana Churchill**
A Parlour-Maid	**Meg Maxwell**
Thane Lampeter	**Anthony Nicholls**
Marian Tillyard	**Ruth Dunning**
Ian	**John Cavanah**
Harold	**John Stratton**
Phyllis	**Dora Bryan**
Daker	**Noel Willman**

Directed by Glen Byan Shaw
Setting by Michael Weight

The first revival of Accolade was presented by Nicola Seed, at the Finborough Theatre, on 1 February 2011 with the following cast:

Will Trenting	**Aden Gillett**
Albert	**Alan Francis**
Rona	**Saskia Wickham**
Thane Lampeter	**Patrick Brennan**
Marian Tillyard	**Emma Jerrold**
Ian	**Patrick Osborne**
Harold	**Simon Darwen**
Phyllis	**Olivia Darnley**
Daker	**Graham Seed**

Directed by Blanche McIntyre
Design by James Cotterill
Lighting Design by Neill Brinkworth
Sound by Edward Lewis

The first performance of this production was presented by Nicola Seed at the St James Theatre, on 12th November 2014 with the following cast:

Will Trenting	**Alexander Hanson**
Albert	**Daniel Crossley**
Rona	**Abigail Cruttenden**
Thane Lampeter	**Jay Villiers**
Marian Tillyard	**Claire Cox**
Ian	**Sam Clemmett**
Harold	**Jay Taylor**
Phyllis	**Olivia Darnley**
Daker	**Bruce Alexander**

Directed by Blanche McIntyre
Design by James Cotterill
Lighting by Peter Mumford
Sound by Emma Laxton

The action of the play takes place in Will Trenting's study,
in his house near Regent's Park, London.

The time is 1950.

Scene One An early morning in January.
Scene Two Three months later. Night.
Scene Three The next morning.

Interval

Scene Four Immediately afterwards.
Scene Five The next morning.
Scene Six Three days later. Late Afternoon.

The performance lasts approximately two hours and thirty minutes.

There will be one interval of twenty minutes.

CREATIVE & PRODUCTION TEAM

PLAYWRIGHT Emlyn Williams
DIRECTOR Blanche McIntyre
DESIGNER James Cotterill
LIGHTING DESIGNER Peter Mumford
SOUND DESIGNER Emma Laxton
CASTING DIRECTORS Gemma Hancock CDG and Sam Stevenson CDG
HAIR AND MAKE UP DESIGNER Betty Marini
PRODUCTION MANAGER Andreas Ayling
STAGE MANAGER Stevie Haighton
ASSISTANT STAGE MANAGER & WARDROBE SUPERVISOR Jennie Quirk
PRODUCTION ELECTRICIAN/PROGRAMMER Gregory Jordan

PRODUCER NICOLA SEED PRODUCTIONS
PRODUCER Nicola Seed
ASSISTANT PRODUCER Jack Maple

ASSOCIATE PRODUCER SNAPDRAGON PRODUCTIONS
PRODUCER Sarah Loader
ARTISTIC DIRECTOR Eleanor Rhode

PRODUCTION CREDITS
Set Construction CAPITAL SCENERY
Makeup supplied by MAC
Lighting supplied by WHITE LIGHT
Sound supplied by AUTOGRAPH
Legal Neil Adleman for HARBOTTLE & LEWIS
Insurance Robert Israel for GORDON & CO.
Accountancy COLLINS AND CO
Rehearsal space ST AGNES, ST GABRIELS
Wallpaper from ANDREW MARTIN www.andrewmartin.co.uk
Panelling from LINCRUSTA www.lincrusta.com
Carpet from REMLAND CARPETS www.remlandcarpets.co.uk

PRESS
Kate Morley PR
www.katemorleypr.com

MARKETING
Martin Gray and Charlotte Ward for EMG Entertainment
www.emg-ents.com

PHOTOGRAPHY
Publicity Photographer Eric Richmond
Rehearsal Photographer Ben Broomfield
Production Photographer Mark Douet

CAST

Bruce Alexander (*Daker*)

Theatre includes: recently *A View from the Bridge* (Liverpool Playhouse), *Ciphers* (Out of Joint), *The White House Murder Case* and *The Company Man* (Orange Tree Theatre), *Plenty* (Sheffield Crucible). Also *Waste, The Tempest* (Almeida Theatre), *Life After Scandal* (Hampstead Theatre), *The Reporter, The History Boys, The Mandate* (National Theatre), *Pravda* (Chichester), *Darwin in Malibu* and *St Joan* (Birmingham), *The Permanent Way* (UK tour and Sydney), as well as ten years with the RSC (including *Written on the Heart, Measure for Measure, All's Well That Ends Well, Duchess of Malfi, Twelfth Night , Merry Wives and Cymbeline*). Best known as Supt Mullett in *A Touch of Frost*, other television work includes *Love and Marriage, A Short Stay in Switzerland, Regicides, Midsomer Murders* and *The Innocents.*
Film includes: *Churchill at War, Tomorrow Never Dies, Ladybird Ladybird, Nostradamus* and *Century.*
Also extensive radio work: most recently *The Stuarts* and *The Once and Future King.*

Sam Clemmett (*Ian Trenting*)

Theatre includes: *Nivelli's War* (The Mac Theatre, Belfast), *Lord of the Flies* (Regent's Park Open Air Theatre), *DNA, Private Peaceful*, and *Blood Brothers* (Norwich Theatre Royal).
Television includes: *Diary of a Snob, Holby City, Our World War, Foyle's War*, and for film, *Survivor* and *Burn the Clock.*

Claire Cox (*Marian Tillyard*)

Theatre includes: *Women, Power and Politics* (Tricycle Theatre), *Macbeth* (Shakespeare's Globe), *The Winslow Boy* (Rose Kingston and tour) *The White Devil* (Menier Chocolate Factory), *The Cracks In My Skin, Henry V* (Royal Exchange Manchester), *The Voysey Inheritance, A Little Night Music* (National Theatre), *House of Desires, Pedro the Great Pretender, The Dog in the Manger, American Soap, Julius Caesar, Love in a Wood, A Servant to Two Masters* (Royal Shakespeare Company) and *Design for Living* (ETT).
Television includes: *Wallander, Spooks, Foyle's War, Poirot, Gil Mayo, Your Mother Should Know, Doctors* and *A Touch of Frost.*
Film includes: *Between Us, The Killing, Luther* and *Shooting Fish.*

Daniel Crossley (Albert)

Theatre includes: *Tonight at 8.30* (ETT), *Putting It Together* (St James Theatre), *Lizzie Siddal* (Arcola Theatre), *Singin' in the Rain* (Chichester Festival Theatre and Palace Theatre), *Me and My Girl*, *A Chorus Line* (Sheffield Crucible), *Kiss of the Spider Woman* (Hull Truck), *Mary Poppins* (National Tour), *Hello Dolly!*, *As You Like It*, *Romeo and Juliet*, *Love's Labour's Lost*, *Desires of Frankenstein*, *A Midsummer Night's Dream*, *Oh! What a Lovely War* and *Where's Charlie* (Regent's Park Open Air Theatre), *Anything Goes* and *Love's Labour's Lost* (National Theatre), *Twelfth Night* (West Yorkshire Playhouse), *Abigail's Party* (Northcott Theatre Exeter), *The Snow Queen* (Derby Theatre), *A Midsummer Night's Dream* (Sprite Productions) *I Really Must Be Getting Off* (White Bear), *Roast Chicken* (Hen and Chickens), *Modern Dance for Beginners* (Etcetara Theatre), *Boyband* (Derby Theatre and Gielgud Theatre), *Fosse* (Prince of Wales Theatre), *Chicago* (Adelphi Theatre), *Fame* (Cambridge Theatre), *Cats* (New London Theatre).

Television includes: *Doctors* (BBC), *The Last Enemy* (BBC), *Coronation Street* (ITV), *Heartbeat* (ITV), *The Royals* (E!).

Film includes: *The Borghilde Project*, *Working Lunge*.

Radio includes: *Sorry Boys You Failed The Audition* (BBC)

Abigail Cruttenden (Rona Trenting)

Theatre includes: *Drawing the Line*, *55 Days* (Hampstead Theatre), *The Seagull* (Headlong), *A Marvellous Year for Plums*, *The Rivals* (Chichester Festival), *Benefactors* (Sheffield Crucible), *When Did You Last See Your Mother* (Trafalgar Studios), *The Knot of the Heart* (Almeida Theatre), *Afterlife*, *Flight* (National Theatre) and *Twelfth Night* (RSC).

Televison includes: *The Outcast*, *Not Going Out*, *Benidorm* (series regular Kate Weedon), *Foyle's War*, *The Robinsons*, *Sword of Honour*, *Sharpe* and *Love On A Branchline*.

Film includes: *The Theory of Everything*, *Charlotte Gray*, *Hideous Kinky* and *P'tang Yang Kipperbang*.

Olivia Darnley *(Phyllis)*

Theatre includes: *Wolf Hall/Bring Up the Bodies* (RSC and Aldwych Theatre), *Pride and Prejudice* (Regent's Park Open Air Theatre), *A Marvellous Year for Plums* (Chichester Festival Theatre), *A Day in the Death of Joe Egg* (Glasgow Citz) *Accolade* and *The Rat Trap* (Finborough), *All My Sons* (Apollo Theatre), *Artist Descending A Staircase* (The Old Red Lion), *A Midsummer Night's Dream*, *Macbeth* (Regent's Park Theatre), *As You Like It* (Sheffield Crucible), *Hay Fever* (Theatre Royal Haymarket), *Arms and The Man* (Salisbury Playhouse) *Private Lives*, *Much Ado about Nothing* (Theatre Royal Bath), Vincent in Brixton (Library Theatre, Manchester), *The Importance of Being Earnest* (Theatre Royal Bath and National Tour), *The Taming of the Shrew* (National Tour), *Northanger Abbey* (York Theatre Royal), *The Little Fir Tree* (Sheffield Theatres) and *Les Liaisons Dangereuses* (Bristol Old Vic).

Television includes: *Titanic, Hughie Green: Most Sincerely , Miss Marple – the Mirror Crack'd, The Inspector Lynley Mysteries, Doctors, Agatha Christie: A Life in Pictures* and *The Five(ish) Doctors Reboot.*

Film includes: *Death Defying Acts.*

Radio includes: *Lost in Mexico.*

Alexander Hanson *(Will Trenting)*

Theatre includes: *Single Spies* (Rose Theatre Kingston), *Stephen Ward* (Aldwych Theatre), *Jesus Christ Superstar* (UK arena tour), *Uncle Vanya, Tonight at 8.30, An Ideal Husband* (Vaudeville Theatre), *A Little Night Music* (Menier Chocolate Factory / Garrick Theatre / Broadway), *Marguerite* (Theatre Royal Haymarket), *The Sound of Music* (London Palladium), *The Merchant of Venice, Troilus and Cressida, Candide, The London Cuckolds, The Villain's Opera* (National Theatre), *Copenhagen* (National Theatre Tour), *Talking to Terrorists, Shallow End* (Royal Court), *Memory of Water, Cracked* (Hampstead Theatre), *We Will Rock You* (Dominion Theatre), *Sunset Boulevard* (Adelphi Theatre), *Arcadia* (Theatre Royal Haymarket) *Enter the Guardsman, Brel* (Donmar), *A Little Night Music, Hayfever* (Chichester Festival Theatre).

Television includes: *London's Burning, The Man Who Crossed Hitler, Lewis, Midsomer Murders, Party Animals, Auf Wiedersehen Pet, Rosemary and Thyme* and *The Last Detective.*

Film includes: *Papadopolous and Sons, Kidulthood, Mauvaise Passe* and *Fellow Traveller.*

Jay Taylor *(Harold)*

Theatre includes: *Wolf Hall/Bring Up the Bodies* (RSC and Aldwych Theatre), *I Heart Peterborough* (Soho Theatre), *A Clockwork Orange* (Glasgow Citz), *Troilus and Cressida, Titus Andronicus* (Shakespeare's Globe) and *Posh – Rough Cuts* (Royal Court).

Television includes: *Silk, Teaboys, Misfits, Sirens, Consuming Passions, Midsomer Murders* and *The Fixer.*

Film includes: *A Fantastic Fear of Everything, Red Tails, Rise of the Footsoldier* and *Donkey Punch.*

Jay Villiers *(Thane Lampeter)*

Trained at The Bristol Old Vic Theatre School.

Theatre includes: *The Winslow Boy* (Old Vic); *Hedda Gabler, In Praise of Love* (Theatre Royal, Northampton); *Titanic - Scenes From The British Wreck Inquiry 1912* (MAC Theatre, Belfast); *Fanta Orange* (The Finborough); *A Midsummer Night's Dream, Hamlet, Much Ado About Nothing* (The Tobacco Factory, Bristol); *Gone To Earth* (Shared Experience); *Barbarians, The Taming Of The Shrew Dead Funny* (Salisbury Playhouse); *Betrayal, The Browning Version* (Bristol OldVic); *Arcadia, The Admirable Crichton* (Chichester); *Mansfield Park, Six Degrees Of Separation* (Crucible Sheffield); *Hamlet, As You Like It, Much Ado About Nothing* (Renaissance Theatre Company); *Ting Tang Mine, Fathers And Sons, Six Characters in Search Of An Author* (National Theatre); *Richard III* (RSC).

Film includes: *The Sea; The Best Exotic Marigold Hotel; The Lady; The International; Before The Rain; Virgin Territory;* and *Henry V.*

Television includes: *Mr Selfridge; Extras; Father Brown; Absolute Power; Lewis; Midsomer Murders; The Leopard Of Rudraprayag; Heartbeat; Spooks; Silent Witness; The Government Inspector; Monsignor Renard; McCallum; The Sculptress; Black Hearts In Battersea; Rumpole; Lipstick On Your Collar; The Young Indiana Jones Chronicles;* and *Miss Marple.*

CREATIVE TEAM

Blanche McIntyre - Director

Blanche was named Best Director at the 2013 TMA UK Theatre Awards (for *The Seagull*), was the winner of the Critics' Circle Award for Most Promising Newcomer and the Off West End Theatre Award for Best Director in 2012, and the inaugural winner of the Leverhulme Bursary for Emerging Theatre Directors in 2009. She is currently Associate Director at Nuffield and was previously Associate Director at Out of Joint in 2010, and Director in Residence at the National Theatre Studio and the Finborough Theatre in 2009.

Directing credits include: *The Comedy of Errors* (Globe), *Tonight at 8.30*, (ETT UK Tour), *The Nutcracker* (Nuffield); *Ciphers* (Out Of Joint UK Tour); *The Birthday Party* (Manchester Royal Exchange); *The Seagull* (Headlong UK Tour/Nuffield); Liar Liar (Unicorn Theatre); *The Only True History of Lizzie Finn* (Southwark Playhouse); *The Seven Year Itch* (Salisbury Playhouse); *Repentance/Behind The Lines* (ANGLE at the Bush Theatre); *Foxfinder, Accolade, Molière* or *the League of Hypocrites* (Finborough Theatre); *When Did You Last See My Mother?* (Trafalgar Studios); *Pinching For My Soul* (Focus Theatre Dublin); *Open Heart Surgery* as part of Theatre Uncut (Southwark Playhouse, Soho Theatre); *Wuthering Heights* (Tour); *The Revenger's Tragedy* (BAC); *The Master and Margarita* (Greenwich Playhouse).

James Cotterill - Designer

Recent designs include: *The Comedy of Errors, Much Ado About Nothing* (Shakespeare's Globe); *Smack Family Robinson* (Rose Theatre); *That Day We Sang, To Kill A Mockingbird, Good, A View from the Bridge,* P*owder Monkey and Mojo Mickybo* (Manchester Royal Exchange); *Moth* (High Tide/Bush Theatre); *Love Your Soldier, Straight, The Pride, That Face* (Sheffield Crucible Studio); *Playing the Games* (Criterion); *The Seven Year Itch* (Salisbury Playhouse); *Early One Morning, Journey's End, Hobson's Choice, Long Day's Journey Into Night, Macbeth, The Demolition Man* (Bolton Octagon); *The Widowing of Mrs Holroyd* (New Vic); *The Flint Street Nativy* (Hull Truck); *Accolade* (Finborough Theatre); *The Wages of Thin* (Old Red Lion - Off West End.Com Nomination for Best Set); *Estate Walls* (Oval House); *Romeo & Juliet*(BAC); *The Eleventh Capital, Gone Too Far!* (Royal Court Upstairs); *Big Sale*(Protein Dance); *Silverland* (Arcola Theatre); *Fair* (Trafalgar Studio 2); *The Musician* (OMAC, Belfast) and *A Little Neck* (Goat & Monkey at Hampton Court Palace).

He was a winner of the Linbury Prize for Stage Design for *Not The End of The World* at Bristol Old Vic.

Peter Mumford - Lighting Designer

Theatre includes: *King Kong* (Global Creatures/Australia); *Ghosts, Stephen Ward, Old Times, Top Hat* (& UK Tour), *Absent Friends, Jumpy, Much Ado about Nothing, The Lion in Winter, The Misanthrope, An Ideal Husband, Carousel, Fiddler on the Roof, Prick Up Your Ears, A View From the Bridge* (West End); *Scenes from an Execution, Twelfth Night, All's Well That Ends Well, The Reporter, The Hothouse* (National Theatre); *The Wolf from the Door, Circle Mirror Transformation, In the Republic of Happiness, Love & Information, Jumpy, Our Private Life, Sucker Punch, Cock, The Seagull* (& Broadway), *Drunk Enough to Say I Love You?, Dying City* (& set design) (Royal Court Theatre); *Other Desert Cities, Pygmalion, The Entertainer, Richard II* (The Old Vic); *Wonderland, The Last of the Duchess* (Hampstead); *The Dark Earth & the Light Sky* (Almeida); *King Lear* (& BAM), *Heartbreak House* (Chichester Festival); *The Same Deep Water as Me* (Donmar Warehouse); *Bull, A Taste of Honey, Betrayal* (Sheffield Theatres); *Testament* (Dublin Theatre Festival).

Opera & Dance includes: *La Traviata, La Cenerentola* (Glyndebourne); *Werther, Madame Butterfly, Faust, Carmen, Peter Grimes, 125th Anniversary Gala* (New York Met); *Manon Lescaut* (Baden Baden); *Eugene Onegin* (LA Opera); *The Soldier's Tale & Pierrot Lunaire* (Chicago Symphony); *Passion* (Minnesota Opera); *The Damnation of Faust, Lucrezia Borgia, Madam Butterfly, Bluebeard's Castle* (ENO); *Carmen* (& set design), *Petrushka* (Scottish Ballet); *Faster, E=mc², Take Five* (Birmingham Royal Ballet); *Il Trovatore* (Paris); *Fidelio, Two Widows, Don Giovanni, The Ring* (Scottish Opera); *Midsummer Marriage* (Chicago Lyric Opera); *Eugene Onegin & The Bartered Bride* (ROH).

Peter recently directed and designed a concert version of *The Ring Cycle* for Opera North. Future work includes *Women on the Verge of a Nervous Breakdown* at the Playhouse Theatre.

Awards include: Olivier Award for Outstanding Achievement in Dance (*The Glass Blew In & Fearful Symmetries*); Olivier Award for Best Lighting (*The Bacchai*); Knight of Illumination Award (*Sucker Punch*) and Helpmann and Green Room Awards (*King Kong*).

www.petermumford.info

Emma Laxton – Sound Designer

Current And Future Credits Include: *Cat On A Hot Tin Roof* (Royal Exchange, Royal And Derngate And Northern Stage).

Theatre Credits Include: *Pitcairn* (Out Of Joint, Chichester Festival Theatre & UK Tour); *Saints* (Nuffield); *The Colby Sisters Of Pittsburgh* (Tricycle Theatre); *Pests* (Clean Break And Royal Court); *Carthage* (Finborough Theatre); *The Blackest Black, #Aiww: The Arrest Of Ai Wei Wei, Lay Down Your Cross, Blue Heart Afternoon* (Hampstead Theatre); *Coriolanus, Berenice, The*

Physicists, Making Noise Quietly, The Recruiting Officer (Donmar Warehouse); *All My Sons, A Doll's House, Three Birds, The Accrington Pals, Lady Windermere's Fan* (Royal Exchange); *Much Ado About Nothing* (Old Vic); *Nut* (National Theatre); *Henry The Fifth* (Unicorn); *Omg!* (Sadlers Wells, The Place & Company Of Angels); *There Are Mountains* (Clean Break, Hmp Askham Grange); *The Promise* (Donmar Warehouse At Trafalgar Studios); *You Can Still Make A Killing* (Southwark Playhouse); *The Sacred Flame* (English Touring Theatre); *Black T-Shirt Collection* (Fuel UK Tour And National Theatre); *Invisible* (Transport UK Tour & Luxemborg); *Much Ado About Nothing* (Wyndhams Theatre, West End), *Precious Little Talent* (Trafalgar Studios), *Where's My Seat, Like A Fishbone, The Whiskey Taster, If There Is I Haven't Found It Yet, 2nd May 1997, Apologia, The Contingency Plan, Wrecks, Broken Space Season, 2000 Feet Away* (Bush Theatre); *Charged* (Clean Break, Soho Theatre); *Men Should Weep* (National Theatre); *My Romantic History* (Sheffield Theatres And Bush Theatre); *Travels With My Aunt* (Northampton Theatre Royal); *Sisters* (Sheffield Theatres); *Pornography* (Birmingham Rep/Traverse And Tricycle Theatre); *Shoot/Get Treasure/ Repeat* (National Theatre); *Europe* (Dundee Rep/Barbican Pit).

Emma is the Associate Sound Designer For The National Theatre's Production of *War Horse* and was previously an Associate Artist at the Bush Theatre. Emma was previously Deputy Head of Sound for the Royal Court where her designs include: *The Westbridge* (Jerwood Theatre Upstairs And Theatre Local), *The Heretic, Off The Endz!, Tusk Tusk, Faces In The Crowd, That Face* (And Duke Of York's Theatre, West End), *Gone Too Far!, Catch, Scenes From The Back Of Beyond*, **Woman And A Scarecrow**, *The World's Biggest Diamond, Incomplete And Random Acts Of Kindness, My Name Is Rachel Corrie (*and Playhouse Theatre, West End and Minetta Lane Theatre, New York And Galway Festival And Edinburgh Festival), *Bone, The Weather, Bear Hug, Terrorism, Food Chain.*

Gemma Hancock CDG and **Sam Stevenson** CDG - Casting Directors

TV work includes: *Our World War, Glasgow Girls* (BBC 3), *Nightshift, Care, The Snipist, The Minor Character* and *Nixon's the One* ('Playhouse Presents' for Sky Arts), *The Selection* (Warner Bros), four series of *Silent Witness* (BBC 1), *Martin Amis' Money* (BBC 2), *Consuming Passion, Mr Loveday's Little Outing* (BBC 4), *The Inspector Lynley Mysteries* (BBC 1), and many episodes of *The Bill* for ITV. In 2010 Gemma and Sam received a Primetime Emmy nomination for their casting of *Emma* for BBC 1.

Film work includes: *Leave to Remain, Private Peaceful, Babel, The New Worl*d.

Theatre work includes: *The Vertical Hour* (Park theatre), *Perseverance Drive, The Herd* (Bush theatre), *One Man, Two Guvnors* (West End and national tour), *55 Days, In the Club, What the Butler Saw, Abigail's Party* (Hampstead theatre), *The Humans* (Rotterdam, New York, Avignon), *Our Country's Good* (St James Theatre and national tour), *The Real Thing* (tour), *Breakfast at Tiffany's, Ring Round the Moon, Waiting for Godot* (West End), Canary (tour), *Tejas Verdes, Emperor Jones, The Chairs* (Gate theatre), *King*

Lear (RSC), *Blood and Gifts* (NT). Sam and Gemma have also cast more than 20 productions for Peter Hall, including *Henry IV, Pygmalion, Where There's A Will, Waiting for Godot, Uncle Vanya, The Dresser, As You Like It, Habeas Corpus and Measure for Measure.*

Betty Marini - Hair and Make-up Designer

Betty trained in Hairdressing, wig making and media make up before starting her career at the RSC in Stratford upon Avon. She has worked extensively for the RSC, Royal Opera House, Royal Ballet and Glyndebourne.

West End and Broadway productions include: *Mary Poppins, The Lion King, Betty Blue eyes, Miss Saigon,* and *Les Miserables,* International Tours include: *French & Saunders, The King & I, Batman International Arena tour, Sir Peter Hall's Tantalus* and *Taboo.*

As a designer, Betty's credits include the wigs and make up design for *Monty Python Live* (O2). Betty was recently Co Supervisor for *The Bodyguard* (Adelphi Theatre). Other supervising work includes: *Black Comedy* (Chichester Festival Theatre), *American Psycho, The Quartermaines Terms, The Pride and Macbeth* (Trafalgar Studios), *Dreamboats and Petticoats, The Prince of Homburg and Night Alive* (Donmar Warehouse), *Evita, Cabaret, Pack of Lies (*UK Tours), *Backbeat* (Los Angeles) and the Olympic Opening and Closing Ceremonies (Athens 2004). Associate Supervisor work includes: *Dirty Dancing* (Milan), *Barnum* (UK Tour) and Assistant Supervisor on *Dirty Rotten Scoundrels.*

Film work includes the upcoming *Cinderella and Spy, I Zombie, The Princess in the Tower* and *Far from the Loved Ones.* Television includes *Dirty work* and *Any Human Heart* (Kim Cattrall's personal supervisor).

Andreas Ayling – Production Manager

Andreas began working professionally in theatre in 2005 as part of the electrics department on *Phantom Of The Opera,* before leaving in 2010 to study Technical & Production Management at Central School of Speech and Drama.

During his studies and subsequently, Andreas has worked for Crosbie Marlow Associates as assistant production manager on *Mamma Mia, Viva Forever* and *Around The World In 80 Days.* Additionally, he has also worked on the UK and Ireland tours of *American Idiot: The Musical* and Oliver!, as well as the *The Phantom Of The Opera* 25th Anniversary Concert at The Royal Albert Hall. After completing his degree, Andreas joined Opera Holland Park, where he has held the position of head of stage & assistant production manager for both the 2013 and 2014 summer seasons. In 2013 Andreas production managed the Xbox One European promotional tour. 2014 has also seen Andreas production manage the highly acclaimed production of *In The Heights* at Southwark Playhouse, as well as join the company of *The Lion King* as a stage dep. He is also currently working on the UK Tours of *Miracle on 34th Street* and *The Full Monty*.

www.andreasayling.com

Stevie Haighton – Stage Manager

Stevie is a graduate of the University of Reading and trained at the Bristol Old Vic Theatre School. Previous productions as stage manager and deputy stage manager include: *Breeders* (St James Theatre), *In the Vale of Health* (Hampstead Theatre); *One Man Two Guvnors* (Theatre Royal Haymarket). She has been stage manager and assistant stage manager for the Menier Chocolate Factory on their productions of *Without You* (Edinburgh Festival), *Educating Rita* (also UK tour), *Pippin*, *Terrible Advice* and *Road Show*. She was assistant stage manager for *Chekhov In Hell* (Soho Theatre) and *Lend Me A Tenor* at the Theatre Royal Plymouth and in the West End. Most recently, she staged managed the International Youth Arts Festival at the Rose Theatre in Kingston. @shaighton

Jennie Quirk – Assistant Stage Manager and Wardrobe Supervisor

Jennie is originally from Swansea, South Wales and graduated from Guildford School of Acting with a BA Hons Degree in Professional Production Skills. She has also completed Level One in Bespoke Tailoring from Newham College.

Recent Wardrobe credits include: Wardrobe Supervisor on *Breeders* (St James Theatre); Wardrobe Assistant on *The Drowned Man*(Punchdrunk); Wardrobe Assistant on *Robbie Williams Live, Swings Both Ways* (London Palladium); Dresser on *The Curious Incident Of The Dog In The Night Time* (National Theatre Productions); Costume Maker for *Grim Tales* (West Glamorgan Theatre); Costume Maker on *Love Sick* (Camden Fringe) and Wardrobe Assistant on *Bingo* (The Young Vic).

Recent Stage Management credits include: ASM/Book cover on *The Woman In Black* (PW Productions Touring Production); *Hysteria*(Theatre Royal Bath/Tour); *Wife Begins At 40* (Yvonne Arnaud Theatre); SM/DSM on *Repentance/Behind The Lines* (The Bush Theatre); CSM/DSM on *When Did You Last See My Mother* (Trafalgar Studios); SM on *We Are Shadows* (Spitalfields Music Festival); ASM on *The Sanctuary Lamp* (The Arcola/ Ireland tour) and CSM on *Accolade* (The Finborough).

PRODUCERS

Nicola Seed - Producer

Nicola formed Nicola Seed Productions Ltd in 2011, to work on independent productions and freelance projects. Productions include, *Drama At Inish* by Lennox Robinson, starring Celia Imrie and Paul O'Grady, and *Too True To Be Good* by Bernard Shaw, as well as the original production of *Accolade* all at the Finborough Theatre. Associate Producer credits include *A Life* by Hugh Leonard, *The Drawer Boy* by Michael Healey.

Prior to this Nicola worked as Production Assistant for Nimax Theatres from 2007 to 2011, assisting on productions including *Swimming With Sharks* starring Christian Slater (Vaudeville Theatre) and *Rain Man* starring Josh Hartnett (Apollo Theatre). She attended the Stage One Workshop for New Producers in 2010 and was awarded a Stage One Bursary for New Producers 2010-2011 for her production of *Accolade* at the Finborough.

Nicola has been a Production Associate of Paul Elliott/Triumph Entertainment and Karl Sydow since 2012, working on the transfers of Backbeat from the West End to Toronto and Los Angeles. Current and recent projects include the 2014 World Tour of *The Last Confession* directed by Jonathan Church and starring David Suchet; the transfer of *Our Country's Good* from St. James Theatre to Toronto, and the international productions of *Dirty Dancing* in Italy, Australia and France. Her freelance projects include roles as the Central Coordinator of the Victory Ceremonies for the London 2012 Olympic Games, Associate General Manager of the Olivier Awards in 2013 and Project Manager of TheatreCraft 2013.

Snapdragon Productions – Associate Producer

Snapdragon Productions was founded in 2009 by Producer Sarah Loader and Artistic Director Eleanor Rhode, to bring neglected and unknown works to new audiences.

Since 2013 Snapdragon have presented three plays at Park Theatre's 200-seat space: a revival of Thark by Ben Travers, adapted by Clive Francis (August 2013), the London premiere of *The Dead Wait* by Paul Herzberg (November 2013) and *Toast* by Richard Bean (August 2014) which broke box office records and earned Snapdragon a nomination for Best Producer in the 2015 Off West End Awards.

Previously Snapdragon enjoyed a extensive collaboration with the Finborough Theatre, where they produced *A Life* by Hugh Leonard (October 2012), *The Drawer Boy* by Michael Healey (July 2012), B*arrow Hill* by Jane Wainwright (August 2012) *Generous* by Michael Healey (2010), Rodgers and Hammerstein's *Me and Juliet* (2010) and *A Day at the Racists* by Anders Lustgarten, which was nominated for the 2010 TMA Award for Outstanding Achievement in Regional Theatre.

Productions in development include a West End revival with QNQ, the World Premieres of *Smolensk* by Sarah Grochala and *The Session* by Andrew Muir, a revival of *A Bill of Divorcement* by Clemence Dane, and a repertory production of *The Talley House*: a trilogy of plays by Lanford Wilson which includes the Pulitzer Prize Winning *Talley's Folly*.

Special Thanks to Stage One and the Stage One Council

FOR THE ONE STAGE SEASON

DESIGN, MARKETING AND PROMOTIONS by AKA

www.akauk.com

PRESS REPRESENTATIVE the Corner Shop PR

www.thecornershoppr.com

PRODUCTION THANKS:

Neil Adleman, Srianti Alwis, Duncan Bell and the team at Autograph, Craig Bennett and the team at Whitelight, James Bierman, Alan Brodie, Marc Brown, Nick Butler, John Causebrook, Michael Collins, Angela Clutton, Natalie Crisp, Emily Dobbs, Gary Donaldson, Julian Edwards, Paul Elliott, Jackie Elton, Amy Gillard, Vicky Graham, Martin Gray, Katie Harper, Lucinda Harvey, Robert Israel, Dean Kilford, Matthew Keeler, Meg Massey, Crosbie Marlow, Neil McPherson - Artistic Director Finborough Theatre, Sarah McNair, Kate Morley, Alex Milward, Pelham Olive, Out of Joint, Jenny Pearce, David Pugh, The Salisbury Public House, Nick Salmon, Emma Selim, Joseph Smith, the team of the St James Theatre, Karl Sydow, Frankie Rose-Taylor, Rebecca Targett, Nicola Tune, Charlotte Ward and Jamie Wilson.

This production is dedicated to the memory of Anthony Field (1928–2014) who provided incredible support and a wealth of information.

FINBOROUGH | THEATRE

"A blazing beacon of intelligent endeavour, nurturing new writers while finding and reviving neglected curiosities from home and abroad." *The Daily Telegraph*

"One of the most stimulating venues in London, fielding a programme that is a bold mix of trenchant, politically thought-provoking new drama and shrewdly chosen revivals of neglected works from the past." *The Independent*

"A disproportionately valuable component of the London theatre ecology. Its programme combines new writing and revivals, in selections intelligent and audacious." *Financial Times*

"The Finborough Theatre has developed a reputation out of all proportion to its tiny size. It has played its part in the careers of many remarkable playwrights, directors, and actors." *Financial Times*

Founded in 1980, the multi-award-winning Finborough Theatre presents plays and music theatre, concentrated exclusively on new writing and genuine rediscoveries from the 19th and 20th centuries. Behind the scenes, we continue to discover and develop a new generation of theatre makers – through our vibrant Literary team, our prestigious internship scheme and our Resident Assistant Director Programme. Many of the Finborough Theatre's productions transfer to the West End and internationally. Previous transfers from the Finborough Theatre to the St James Theatre include London Wall by John Van Druten. Like London Wall, this production of Accolade was originally rediscovered for the Finborough Theatre by Artistic Director Neil McPherson.

www.finboroughtheatre.co.uk

Accolade

by Emlyn Williams

FOR AMATEUR PRODUCTION ENQUIRIES

UNITED KINGDOM AND WORLD EXCLUDING NORTH AMERICA
plays@SamuelFrench-London.co.uk
020 7255 4302/01
UNITED STATES AND CANADA
info@SamuelFrench.com
1-866-598-8449
Each title is subject to availability from Samuel French,
depending upon country of performance.

THE CHARACTERS

(In order of their appearance)

WILL TRENTING

ALBERT (his valet-chauffeur)

RONA (his wife)

A PARLOUR-MAID

THANE LAMPETER

MARIAN TILLYARD

IAN (son of Will and Rona Trenting)

HAROLD

PHYLLIS (his wife)

DAKER

Scene One

WILL TRENTING's *study, in his house in Regent's Park, London. The time is the present: an early morning in January.*

In the left wall (throughout the play 'left' and 'right' refer to the audience's left and right), the fireplace, downstage (with in front an electric fire); in the left wall, upstage, a door leading to the kitchen quarters (throughout, this door is called the kitchen door). In the back wall, more or less in the centre, a door (called, throughout, the main door) leading to the hall, which branches to left and right; on the left it leads to the drawing-room and dining-room, on the right to the front door. Just in sight (framed by the main doorway) the staircase leads up to the left. In the right wall, downstage, French windows lead to a London garden.

Salient furniture is disposed as follows. Below the fireplace, against the left wall, a small desk with a chair (RONA'S desk); in front of the fireplace, a low stool; facing the audience just beyond the fireplace, on the left side of the stage, a comfortable old sofa; behind it the drinks table; roughly in the middle of the room, a small arm-chair; on the right side of the stage, a large flat desk with a desk chair behind it, its back to the window (on the desk, a telephone and a reading lamp); a small light baize-covered table, with a typewriter on it (called the typing table) which is moved about during the action (with this table goes a small chair, which when not in use can be put away into the gap of the desk); against the right wall, below the windows, a low cupboard; in the corner between the back wall and the right wall, a corner cupboard with doors, which contains a roughly fitted wardrobe, wash basin and

1

small shaving cupboard. Over the low cupboard to the right, a framed French painting; another over the mantelpiece. On RONA'S desk, a small portable radio set, and a framed photograph. Against the bookshelves at the back, to the left of the main door, library steps.

The room is attractively furnished and decorated (in the way of curtains, carpets and covers) by a wife who has adapted her taste to suit a man's room, intending the result to please without being elegant. It is a comfortable sitting-room, but could never be taken for the drawing-room; it is small and intimate, and primarily the workroom of a professional writer who has unconsciously accumulated around him, over the years, a litter of personal objects. One guesses that he is exuberantly untidy; the walls are almost hidden by shelves bursting with books and periodicals, which overflow on to the mantlepiece and floor; the desk top is a welter of papers and writer's paraphernalia.

The curtains are open; the sunshine from the garden is unmistakably winter morning light, but cheerful. The main door is open; the typing table is in front of the desk, next to the typewriter is an open press-cutting book, on it a pile of loose cuttings.

A pause: **WILL** *wanders downstairs. He looks into the hall, to the right, and wanders through the main doorway into the room; he is in his dressing-gown, pyjamas and slippers.*

WILL TRENTING *is in the forties, with an unusual combination of physical and mental vigour; he radiates animal health as a child does (with, mixed in the current, strong and unconscious sexuality) while the flexible and enthusiastic temper of his mind is that of a brilliantly attractive child. He has no interest in his looks; his hair is on end like a schoolboy's, his pyjamas are rumpled, his dressing gown old and serviceable. His innate and natural modesty (almost a diffidence) would, however, prevent anybody mistaking him for an irritating Bohemian.*

He is at the moment in a state of subdued thoughtful excitement; he looks at his wristwatch, and peers out of the windows, trying to see over the garden wall. He sees the open press-cutting book, picks it up, and glances at the cuttings, smiling; he crosses to the fireplace, turns on the electric fire, and sits on **RONA***'s desk chair, with the press cutting book on his knee, to examine the cuttings.*

ALBERT *enters briskly by the kitchen door; he is smoking, and carries a sheaf of typing paper. He is a Londoner, in the middle thirties, with a pleasant quiet manner, who manages to have a permanent twinkle in his eye and yet remain the correct servant; he wears a dark suit. He closes the kitchen door, takes the cover off the typewriter, whistling, sits at the typing table and types a word or two.* **WILL** *makes a restless movement, and* **ALBERT** *realises he is in the room.*

ALBERT. Sorry, sir… Happy New Year.

WILL. Happy New Year, Albert – the papers are very late, aren't they?

ALBERT. I expect the paper-boy's got a hangover.

WILL. Never thought of that… what are you on?

ALBERT. Chapter Four, sir, the new corrections.

He continues to type.

A sharp rat-tat-tat at the front door; **WILL** *looks at* **ALBERT***, who stops typing and looks up at him.* **WILL** *lays the book on the stool, goes to the main door, opens it, looks towards the front door, and goes to the stairs.*

WILL. *(calling up the stairs)* Rona!

He disappears to the right; **ALBERT** *rises, takes up the typing table, and carries it towards the main door;* **WILL** *reappears carrying three morning newspapers.*

ALBERT. *(smiling)* I'll take this into the dining-room, sir.

He goes off into the hall, to the left; **WILL** *hurries down, sits in* **ALBERT***'s chair, extracts* The Times, *and turns the pages spasmodically. He finds what he is looking for.*

*He stares at it, with a mixture of pleasure and shyness;
then folds the paper ready.*

RONA *comes down the stairs and in at the main door; she
is a pretty woman, between thirty-five and forty-five, in a
dressing gown and slippers. Without* **WILL** *'s unconsciously
dominating personality, she is as spontaneous. They are
husband and wife who have loved each other long enough
to forget about it most of the time.*

RONA. Darling, you *are* starting the New Year off restless –
aren't you cold?

(closing the main door, and moving towards the kitchen.)
I asked her to call us late, would you like some
tea? *(as he turns, slowly, and looks at her)* What is it?

WILL. I've got a present for you.

RONA. But I've already had my Christmas present –

WILL. Every New Year, his Majesty bestows honours on
various loyal subjects.
Didn't you know? *(holding out the paper)*

RONA. But what… *(she takes the paper, looks down at this, sees
something, then looks up at* **WILL**, *incredulously)* You've
been knighted.

WILL. Yes.

RONA. *(bewildered)* But you'd have told me –

WILL. You have to promise the gent at Buckingham Palace
to keep it from anybody who might blab.

RONA. Of course… but my dearest, you're a *Sir*… *(reading
from the paper)* 'For Services to Literature'… What a
wonderful wonderful thing…

They embrace, spontaneously, fondly.

WILL. My darling…

RONA. How right he was, I'd have told everybody! *(looking
from the paper to him again, with realisation.)* But it turns
me into a Lady…

WILL. It does.

RONA. But isn't that *amazing – (as the telephone rings) –* it's started, the whole of London's on to us – I can't talk to anybody yet, not till I've taken it in –

She switches off the telephone, as **ALBERT** *enters by the kitchen door, carrying a suit of* **WILL**'s *on a hanger. The telephone is heard ringing, faintly in the drawing-room.*

Albert, we've got news –

WILL. *(rising)* He knew weeks ago, he opened the letter. *(he crosses to the fireplace;* **ALBERT** *goes to the cupboard and hangs the hanger inside it)*

RONA. And you both kept it under your hats, *well... (to* **WILL***)* So *that's* why you've been insisting on people coming in for drinks crack-of-dawn New Year's Day – but they'll be here any second, I must finish dressing –

WILL. Not for a minute –

RONA. All right... *(as the telephone stops ringing, in the drawing-room)* Albert, tell Gladys to tell anybody who rings up –

ALBERT. She's answering it in the drawing-room. I said to say you're not in till eleven, was that right?

RONA. Perfect...

ALBERT. *(remembering something)* My lady –

RONA. *(turning round as if somebody were at the door)* Oh... You mean *me?*

WILL *laughs;* **ALBERT** *giggles, discreetly.*

ALBERT. *New York Times* rang up earlier on, my lady, an' will ring back lunch-time. They want your reaction.

RONA. *(delighted)* My reaction? Bored to tears, gone back to bed! *(looking at* The Times*)* The *faces* of people when they see this!

ALBERT *goes out by the kitchen door;* **RONA** *leaves the paper on the arm-chair.*

WILL. "Trenting the Tramp knighted, what's the country coming to?"

The telephone is heard ringing again, in the distance.

RONA. I can hear the phone in the drawing-room, it's never going to stop, oh dear how lovely… *(looking at him)* Will, you didn't accept just to give me a wonderful surprise? *(the telephone stops ringing)*

WILL. Good lord, no, there's a snob corner of me that's tickled to death, you should have seen me grab at that paper – *(sitting on the sofa)*

RONA. I know, but if you weren't married, would you have accepted?

WILL. *(hesitating)* Well…

RONA. I've suddenly remembered… *(sitting next to him)* That night when you couldn't sleep – and then went off on that binge – *that* was when you had to decide, wasn't it?

WILL. Yes –

RONA. And you accepted, for me…

They kiss.

WILL. *(grinning)* I'm as pleased as Punch, mostly. I just don't feel respectable enough for it – I'm… embarrassed, d'you know what I mean?

RONA. Falstaff was a knight.

WILL. That's a thought.

   ALBERT *returns from the kitchen, carrying a tray with an opened half-bottle of champagne and two filled glasses.*

RONA. Albert, you are wicked…

WILL. He's quite right, we've got to do it properly –

RONA. *(lifting her glass, to* **WILL***)* Darling, to us.

WILL. *(clinking her glass with his)* And Ian –

RONA. Ian. To us, Albert –

   She drinks, then holds out her glass to **ALBERT***, with perfect propriety, he takes a sip, and gives back the glass.*

   Tell Gladys, we won't bother with tea or coffee, just the champagne and the sandwiches… *(as* **ALBERT** *goes* *towards the kitchen door)* Oh and Albert, will you send a wire to my Aunt Millie, 'Will knighted, love writing'.

ALBERT. Yes, my lady.

He turns and goes out by the main door, closing it behind him.

WILL. She'll have a fit.

RONA. *(sitting back)* Oh… *(reminiscent, as* **WILL** *takes her hand)* When that first book came out. We never bargained on this!

WILL. Look, Albert's putting in the old reviews… *(taking up the book, and turning pages)*

RONA. Think of those digs, us in that frosty bed smothered in newspapers, crying –

WILL. Who was crying? *I* wasn't!

RONA. On my shoulder.

WILL. I don't remember that.

RONA. *(reading from a cutting)* 'Cesspool of Novel Calls itself Art'.

WILL. *(pointing and reading)* 'As indecent as badly written'.

RONA. That's the bit that made you cry.

WILL. *(turning a page)* Then they get better –

RONA. Let's gloat. *(picking up one of the cuttings, and reading)* 'Uncanny insight into lower depths'. *(looking at another)* That was when the magazine begged you to cut out the bad house in Portsmouth, remember? Thank God you didn't… *(turning a page)* 'Will Trenting wins Nobel Prize'. Mmm…

WILL. *(reading from another cutting)* 'His own spiritual glow'. *(grinning at her)* See?

RONA. *(raising her glass)* This has a glow too, why don't we do it every morning. *(drinking, then seeing the low cupboard below the window, which makes an idea come to her)* Oh! *(rising, and crossing to the cupboard)* And now for *my* present –

WILL. Yours?

RONA. It was for our anniversary, but here goes…

> *She takes out a heavy object and lays it on the desk; it is a bookstand holding ten uniform volumes, beautifully bound.*

WILL. But what – *(going to look)* – they're mine!

RONA. The Works Of.

WILL. *(like a child)* But I've never seen anything so handsome –

RONA. *(sliding the books round so that they face the desk chair)* They do look rather nice, don't they…

WILL. And they're the perfect present for this morning –

RONA. There! *(as they kiss, impulsively, across the desk)* We've got Ian, and each other, and this – oh dear, it's going to my head.

> *The* **PARLOUR-MAID** *opens the main door, a man's overcoat over one arm.*

THE MAID. *(announcing)* Mr Lampeter.

> **THANE** *enters by the main door; the* **MAID** *closes the door from the outside.* **THANE**, *a contemporary of* **WILL***'s, has the manner of a sophisticated barrister, with behind it a first-class realistic brain, untarnished by sentimentality, yet warmed by kindly tolerance.*

RONA. Thane!

WILL. Come in – *(taking his own glass to the drinks table, filling it, and coming down to the fireplace)*

THANE. *(going to* **RONA***)* Sir William's publisher has been proud to raid his own Christmas roses. (*holding out a bunch of flowers*)

RONA. You shouldn't have – *(taking them)*

THANE. But what a spectacular was of bringing in the New Year! *(crossing in front of the sofa, and taking the glass from* **WILL***)* You'll never top *this* in the next twelve months… *(shaking him by the hand)* I'm proud of you.

WILL. That's pretty generous, Thane, when you think you should have been given it two years ago –

THANE. *(sitting on the sofa):* But I saw their point- who wants to knight a dreary old bachelor because he's married to an enormous harem of books and gets his fun from publishing them? *(as* **RONA** *kisses the back of his head)* Nonsense, you're a family man, that's when it's worth something... *(to* **RONA***)* You'll find yourself on a few committees now, my girl.

RONA is at the washstand, filling a small vase with water for the flowers.

WILL. Committees? Oh lord –

RONA. It'll be rather fun, being a bit grand...

The main door bursts open, and **MARIAN TILLYARD** *hurries in, carrying a newspaper. She is an attractive intelligent woman of* **RONA***'s age, and fairly typical of their mutual friends; she has a warm unaffected personality, while remaining more conventional than* **RONA**. **THE PARLOUR-MAID** *closes the main door from the outside.*

MARIAN. *(excited, rapping* **WILL** *on the shoulder with the newspaper)* Trenting the Tramp, I dub thee knight- isn't it *thrilling*, where's me lady?

RONA. You may kiss my hand, riff-raff – *(embracing her)* – I'm so glad you two are the first –

MARIAN. I woke up to find the charwoman shaking me and brandishing the *Daily Mirror*, I tore out of the flat – *(to* **RONA***)* – do me up, sweetie... Thane, what *about* all this?

WILL has taken a shaving brush from the washstand and is studying his present, at the desk. **ALBERT** *comes in by the kitchen door, carrying a tray with a second (opened) bottle of champagne and two glasses; he pours champagne.*

WILL. *(worried)* Thane, I won't be expected to go around opening bazaars in a pair of spats?

MARIAN. *(laughing)* The Tramp in spats, I'd stand in line for that! *(To* **ALBERT***, taking her glass, and sitting on the sofa.)* Happy New Year, Albert, what wonderful news –

WILL. But I've never made a speech in my life, it would terrify me –

MARIAN. I remember one you made, love.

WILL. When was that?

THANE. The time I coaxed you on to the air.

WILL. Don't…

MARIAN. On the Brains Trust, *on* a Sunday, when you called Lord Beal a hypocritical old maid.

RONA. *(sitting, next to her)* That's not fair, he was so nervous he'd had some rum.

WILL. I should never drink rum –

He hurries out by the main door and upstairs, followed by **ALBERT***, who closes the door behind them.*

MARIAN. *(raising her glass)* To Sir William –

RONA. *(raising her glass to* **THANE***)* Sir William's publisher…

They drink.

MARIAN. 'Sir' – but it doesn't go with our Will at *all!* Makes it all the more perfect…

RONA. Oh dear, I hope so…

MARIAN. Why 'oh dear'?

RONA. You know how he's always fought like a steer against anything that tied him down.

MARIAN. You mean he won't like not going by bus, and all that?

RONA. *(alarmed):* But surely they won't expect –

THANE. His mother would never have let Sir William go by bus.

RONA. I'm glad she didn't live to see this, is that awful of me?

MARIAN. Was she a rod of iron?

RONA. *And* killed him with kindness. Dressed him in a velvet suit.

MARIAN. Literally?

RONA. Literally. *(sipping)* If she'd had her way he'd still be wearing it. It made him allergic to velvet. That's why he got tight before that broadcast – the letters 'B.B.C' just spelt 'Mother' to him and he flew to the rum. Took me right back –

ALBERT comes in by the main door.

ALBERT. Mr. and Mrs. Wickram and Miss Lett, my lady, I've showed them in the drawing-room –

RONA. *(rising)* The party's on! *(to the others.)* I'll be with you – *(to ALBERT)* – is there champagne for them?

ALBERT. I took it in earlier, my lady –

RONA hurries out by the main door, almost colliding with WILL as he hurries downstairs and into the room, carrying his razor. He goes to the washstand and fixes a blade into it.

RONA. *(back in the doorway, an afterthought)*: And Albert, switch the phone back on, will you, nobody'll be able to hear a thing in there –

She hurries upstairs. ALBERT switches on the telephone.

MARIAN. *(suddenly touched, clapping her hands)*: Even the flowers smell of success! I'm so happy for the three of you...

She kisses WILL, on the back of the head, impulsively.

WILL. Thank you Marian –

MARIAN runs out by the main doorway to the left.

MARIAN. Did you say the Wickrams, Albert?

ALBERT. *(following her)* Yes, madam –

He closes the main door, behind them. For the last minute, standing at the fireplace, THANE has been watching WILL, thoughtfully. WILL turns, as he is about to shave, and catches his eye.

WILL. You're looking very knowing.

THANE. I was thinking of your reputation.

A pause. **WILL** *turns to him.*

WILL. My reputation?

THANE. Odd how impressive a symbol can still be. Even such an antiquated one as knighthood… Oh, your reputation is just right. Just as a rumour starts about Trenting the Tramp, we see his wife, son and garden beautified in the *Tatler*. You get it both ways. It's a golden moment. *(toasting* **WILL***)*

WILL. You mean it won't last?

THANE. You'll find yourself being watched.

WILL. That sounds sinister.

THANE. *(smiling)*: No no – I mean as a public person is watched. For a lead in proper behaviour.

WILL. Proper? But what has a word like 'proper' got to do with anything I ever put on paper –

THANE. I'm not thinking of your writing, I mean your private life.

WILL. *(after a pause)*: Thane…*(designating the newspaper)*… this is making me put you a question. Since I've been married, what exactly do you know of my private life?

THANE. *(after a pause)*: Nothing definite.

IAN comes in by the main door, leaving it open. He is a schoolboy of thirteen to fourteen, young for his age: a callow sensitive creature, but his shyness is pleasant and unselfconscious. He is in old holiday clothes (a sweater, no jacket) and carries an open book. WILL sits on the sofa, thoughtfully.

IAN. Happy New Year… *(excited)* Dad, I've got to the last sentence of *Edwin Drood!*

WILL. Oh, too bad –

THANE. Is it as good as I told you?

RONA comes downstairs and into the room; she has changed into a dress. WILL takes his glass of champagne from the table.

WILL. And when you think nobody'll ever know how Dickens meant it to end!

IAN. Because Dickens died, Mummy, in the middle of a sentence!

RONA. I know.

IAN. You do?… Shall I show you the last seven words he wrote?

RONA. Yes, let's have two minutes, just ourselves – *(sitting on the sofa, as* IAN *sits eagerly between her and* WILL*)* – don't go, Thane – *(to* IAN*, as* THANE *shakes his head and goes tactfully out by the main door, taking his glass and closing the door)* – darling, a chunk of news, Daddy's a knight!

IAN. I know, Albert told me. *(reading)* 'And Then Falls To With An Appetite'. Then Dickens died. Isn't it terrible?

WILL. Terrible. *(toasting* RONA*, then putting his glass to* IAN*'s lips)*

RONA. Just a sip –

WILL. *(as* IAN *tries to take a gulp)* No no – seriously, old boy, skip it, skip it –

RONA. And take a little interest!

IAN. *(concerned)*: Sorry, Dad, I didn't mean to be snooty. As a matter of fact, I'm impressed.

RONA. Daddy wasn't annoyed with you, it's just that he's shy of it at first –

WILL. *(brightening)*: I'll get used to it.

IAN. What does it make me, a baronet?

WILL. Sorry, Trenting Esquire.

IAN. That's a blow, isn't it, Lady Trenting?

RONA. Lady Trenting… it does sound pretty –

IAN. Seriously, Dad, what have they knighted you *for?*

RONA. They knighted Dickens!

IAN. No they didn't.

RONA. Didn't they? Well, they ought to have.

IAN. He was the champion of the poor and Queen Victoria hated his guts, did you know?

WILL. We must assume her great-grandson doesn't mind mine.

RONA. Which does make it rather exciting, don't you think Ian?

IAN. Dad, why haven't you finished *Edwin Drood*?

WILL. How can I, when the author died in the middle?

IAN. I mean finish *writing* it.

WILL. I have my work cut out finishing writing my own.

IAN. Oh… And you'd never be able to do his style, would you?

WILL. I don't expect so.

> **MARIAN** *hurries in by the main door, carrying her glass.*

MARIAN. Hurry up, darlings, they're clamouring for you –

RONA. Just coming –

WILL. (to Ian): You know *why* Dickens died, don't you?

IAN. Why?

WILL. *(pointing to* **IAN**'s *book)* One of the chapters starts with a quotation!

IAN. What is it?

WILL. I daren't repeat it, it's from *Macbeth*.

RONA. Does it really?

WILL. Yes it does –

RONA. *(to* **IAN***)* And *Macbeth's* the unluckiest thing ever written.

IAN. *(fascinated)* And Dickens *died*? Mummy, would something awful happen to Dad if I said 'All the perfumes of Arabia – '

RONA. *(half laughing, half alarmed)*: Don't finish it!

IAN. I stopped before the verb, so Dad's reprieved.

> *He rises, goes to the bookshelves at the back, and climbs the library steps to replace* **EDWIN DROOD** *and take another book.*

MARIAN. *(to* **WILL***)* Come on, I'll announce you…

WILL. *(rising)* All right –

MARIAN. *(taking him by the hand)*: Straighten your white tie and tails, dearie –

She takes him through the main doorway and to the left. **RONA** *kisses* **IAN** *lightly on the head and follows them, closing the main door behind her.* **IAN** *is alone; he climbs down, sits on the sofa and puts his feet up, to read.*

MARIAN'S VOICE. *(outside the drawing-room door, a mock pompous announcement):* Sir… William… Trenting!

The sound of the drawing-room door opening; in the drawing-room, laughter and applause. **IAN**, *engrossed in his book, hears nothing.*

A pause. **ALBERT** *comes in by the main doorway, smiling to himself, with over his arm a pile of furs, overcoats and hats.*

ALBERT. Move up, old chap.

IAN. *(taking his feet off)*: Sorry… Albert, which book d'you think's the best, *Bleak House* or *Great Expectations*?

ALBERT. *(arranging coats on the sofa)* Can't say, was there ever a film of *Bleak House*?

He starts to go. The telephone rings: he answers it.

(the perfect servant): Wellbeck 9732, Sir William Trenting's house… Well he's engaged at the moment, can I help you?… This is his sec'et'ry speakin'… Albert, that's right, could you leave a name, please?… *(descending the social scale, audibly)* Oh yes, I've heard the guv'nor talk about you, haven't I… Oh – *(as we hear a burst of laughter from the drawing-room)* – just a minute – *(going to the main door closing it, and coming back to the telephone)* – he's got a party on at the moment of writin', you see an'… Yurs, it's a great honour, we're tickled to death this end – now could *I* help you?… *(cautiously)* I got a faint idea, yes… Oh. *(sharply)* What's happened?… *(his face and manner sobering)* Oh… Well that's a pretty kettle o' fish, an' no mistake… (**IAN** *looks up*) … I will, I'll get him to ring you… Bye-bye. *(replacing the receiver, in serious thought)*

IAN. Anything happened to Dad?

ALBERT. No, fathead. Your Dad's having a drink in the drawing-room.

IAN. I never got to the verb.

ALBERT. What verb?

IAN. *(going back to his reading)* 'Sweeten'. *Macbeth.*

> ALBERT *shakes his head, uncomprehendingly, and turns to go. He looks down at the telephone, worried, then goes out by the main door.*
>
> *From the drawing-room, a loud burst of laughter.* ALBERT *shuts the main door;* IAN *turns a page, engrossed. The curtain falls, and rises immediately on*

Scene Two

Three months later; night.

The lamps are lit, the curtains are closed, and there is a fire. WILL *sits at his desk, in shirt-sleeves and pullover, thoughtful, pencil in hand, sheets of foolscap before him; he is wearing horn-rimmed glasses.* ALBERT *sits in front of the desk, at his own typing table, typing from a manuscript. At one end of the sofa* RONA *sits knitting a pullover, while* IAN *sits at the other end, reading; he is in his pyjamas, slippers and dressing-gown,* RONA *wears a housecoat.* WILL'*s jacket lies near the desk.*

On a hanger hooked over the wardrobe cupboard, a morning suit: tail-coat and striped trousers. A coffee tray; cups and saucers.

THE PARLOUR-MAID *enters from the kitchen, collects: coffee cups, and takes the tray.*

RONA. Thank you, Gladys. That'll be all, goodnight.

THE PARLOUR MAID. Goodnight –

RONA. Say goodnight, Ian.

IAN. *(without looking up)*: Sorry – goodnight.

THE PARLOUR-MAID. Good-night.

WILL. *(without looking up, as the* **MAID** *reaches the kitchen door)* Good-night.

The **MAID** *goes, closing the kitchen door behind her.* **ALBERT** *stops typing, leans over to* **WILL**, *and shows him something in the script.*

'Discernment'? One 's', one 'c'.

ALBERT. Thank you, sir.

RONA. A'c'? I never knew that.

She leans over, straightens **IAN**'s *arm, measures the pullover along it, and goes on knitting.* **IAN** *has taken no notice; he gives a sigh of delight at what he is reading, looks at the clock, and turns the page.*

No, it's the end of the chapter –

IAN. But you said it was my first night home from school –

RONA. You've already had an extra half an hour, and a big day tomorrow.

IAN. But Lady Dedlock's just going to shoot Mr. Tulkinghorn!

RONA. She'll have to put it off till breakfast.

*   **ALBERT** *finishes typing and covers the machine. The telephone rings; he answers it.*

ALBERT. *(into the telephone)* Wellbeck 9732, Sir William Trenting's house…

RONA. *(to* **WILL**, *as he sighs and crosses out something)* Sorry I should have lit the drawing-room fire –

WILL. It's all right, darling… *(smiling at* **IAN** *)…* I'm trying to finish a chapter too.

ALBERT. *(into the telephone)* Yes, I will – *(to* **RONA** *)* – it's Mrs. Tillyard, my lady, can Ian come to the Crazy Gang, Friday, in her box.

*   **RONA** *looks at* **IAN**, *who does not stir; she nods at* **ALBERT**. *(into the telephone)* Delighted, ta-ta for now. *(hanging up)*

RONA. Albert, did you really say 'ta-ta'?

ALBERT. It was the maid, my lady.

IAN. *(looking up)* What was that?

RONA. Crazy Gang.

IAN. Oh, good.

> *He goes on reading.*
>
> *Almost simultaneously,* **RONA** *and* **ALBERT** *turn towards the windows.*

RONA. Did *you* hear something, Albert?

ALBERT. Sounded like gravel against the window.

RONA. Couldn't be.

> *She goes on knitting,* **ALBERT** *crosses and peers between the curtains. He sees somebody outside, and turns to make sure that none of the other three are looking.*

ALBERT. Nobody there, but I'll just look round –

> *He opens one window, and goes out, closing it behind him.* **WILL** *makes a correction in his script.*

RONA. *(to him)* Don't work too late, dear. *(to* **IAN***)* We can't have him at the Palace with circles under his eyes, can we?

IAN. Is Dad coming to the Crazy Gang, too?

RONA. *(patiently)* Not Victoria Palace, Buckingham.

IAN. Oh yes... *(going back to his book)*

> **ALBERT** *returns, closing the window behind him; he looks thoughtful. He lifts the hanger from the cupboard.*

RONA. *(to* **IAN***)* I've told you four times, he's going in the morning to be invested or given the accolade or whatever it's called. Isn't it lucky you're just home for it? *(seeing the morning suit)* Very smart. Does it fit him?

ALBERT. Perfect my lady. They always make you try on before they hire out.

RONA. *(as* **IAN** *turns a page, quietly)* Up you go, Master Trenting –

IAN. *(to* **WILL**, *closing his book and rising)* You'll come up and say good-night, won't you?

WILL. Of course I will, I'll just finish this paragraph –

IAN. *(as* **ALBERT** *opens the main door)* Good-night, Albert.

ALBERT. Good-night, Ian. I'll help you unpack i' the morning.

IAN. Thank you –

He goes out by the main door and upstairs.

RONA. *(to* **WILL**, *rising and putting away her knitting)* I'll call you when he's in bed – I shan't be long myself. A drink, darling?

WILL. I don't think so. I'll tell you what I *would* like, later – a glass of milk.

RONA. Good idea, make you sleep. *(as* **WILL** *sighs)* Don't worry about Chapter Three, it'll suddenly come to you.

WILL. Thank you, love.

They kiss, fondly; **RONA** *goes out by the main door, and upstairs.* **ALBERT** *shuts the main door, hangs up the morning suit, and comes to* **WILL***.*

ALBERT. Excuse me, sir.

WILL. *(writing)* Yes?

ALBERT. Harold and Phyllis, sir.

WILL. *(looking up, perplexed)* Harold and – *(realising, and beaming)* – Harold and Phyllis! But ask them in! *(taking off his spectacles and rising, as* **ALBERT** *crosses to the windows and opens one)* What are they doing in the garden?

ALBERT. *(calling softly)*: O.K... *(turning to* **WILL***)* they didn't want to come to the door, sir.

WILL. But I never heard such – *(calling outside, affectionately)* – well, and what's the idea of skulking round the house, for God's sake, scaring the pants off Albert here – come in!

HAROLD *comes in by the French windows, followed by* **PHYLLIS**. *They are an attractive pair, both in person and in personality, for they have in common youth (both being in their late twenties) and an unashamed*

*preoccupation with enjoyment. They are two vicious
children who take vice for granted. Both spring from the
lower class (Cockney), have not sprung far, and would
consider wasted any effort to spring further. He wears
a rain-coat, she a beret and tweed-coat; he looks like a
chauffeur off duty, she a nicely dressed barmaid. Both
have been drinking, but are sobered for the moment by
their surroundings; they are almost shy.*

HAROLD. How's tricks, Bill –

PHYLLIS. Bill love, are you mad at us buttin' in?

WILL. *(embracing her)*: Well, this is a surprise –

PHYLLIS. I know –

WILL. Albert, give 'em a drink, will you?

PHYLLIS. What a lovely place, isn't it, Harold?

HAROLD. *(as **ALBERT** pours out drinks)*: Super, yes –

WILL. But what's the matter with the front door?

*He has taken **PHYLLIS**'s arm and sat her on the sofa.
He is completely natural and at home with them: almost
more so that we have yet seen him. One can see that when
HAROLD and **PHYLLIS** are relaxed and in their natural
surroundings, they are three happy topers together.*

HAROLD. Well, we figured you might have some posh do on,
so we got Albert out, to find out the lay o' the land, see –

WILL. D'you mean to say you two have gone all shy on *me?*

PHYLLIS. Well, you're in the Court Circular now, dear –

WILL. I should think I am, and don't you forget it – I'm an
aristoscratchit now!

*(as **PHYLLIS** giggles delightedly)* Well, what news of the
gang?

RONA'S VOICE. *(calling from upstairs)* Ready!

WILL. *(calling)*: Coming! *(to the others)* Just want to say
goodnight to Ian, shan't be a tick…

He runs out of the main door and upstairs.

PHYLLIS. *(sobered, as **ALBERT** shuts the main door)* Of course,
Ian's their little boy, isn't he…*(as **ALBERT** pours her a*

drink) So you're Albert, we've chatted on the phone, haven't we, you're even nicer than your voice.

ALBERT. *(grinning)*: Thanks a lot.

HAROLD. New Year's Day we rang up, wasn't it.

ALBERT. *(non-committedly)*: That's right.

A pause. **HAROLD** *and* **PHYLLIS** *exchange a look.* Drink?

HAROLD. Thanks –

He takes his glass, **ALBERT** *gives* **PHYLLIS** *hers.*

PHYLLIS. Oh Albert, I'll be cock-eyed, we been in the local to get some Dutch courage an' we got on to gin-and-beer – I hope Rona isn't about, hark at me callin' her Rona...

ALBERT. She's quite likely gone to bed.

PHYLLIS. Good. I'd feel awkward. It's psychological.

HAROLD. What does that mean, duck?

PHYLLIS. Haven't a clue – *(giggling)* – cheers! *(drinking, then looking round)* What a glamorous joint.

ALBERT. Different from the old Blue Lion, I bet.

HAROLD. The Blue Lion, Rotherhithe's a smashin' pub, an' don't you believe any opposite.

PHYLLIS. *(to* **ALBERT***)*: Why don't you come down to Rotherhithe one day?

ALBERT. I'm a *West* End type meself.

PHYLLIS. Rotherhithe isn't the East End, it's a sort o' suburb on the river –

HAROLD. A bit slummy, but smashin' pubs... Phyl, take a dekker a the books.

PHYLLIS. Fancy bein' locked in an' havin' to read 'em all, ugh... *(shuddering and drinking)* Albert, has *he* read many?

ALBERT. He wrote some. *(pointing to the edition on the desk)* Those.

PHYLLIS. Oh yes o'course – *isn't* he a funny chap...

HAROLD. *(who has lifted the hanger and draped the morning suit in front of himself)*: D'you fancy me in this, Phyl?

PHYLLIS. Like the news-reels, isn't it?

ALBERT. *(taking the hanger)* I got to press it for the mornin'.

HAROLD. Where's he off too, weddin'?

ALBERT. No, Just droppin' in on the King.

He goes out by the kitchen door.

HAROLD. *(with a laugh)*: Albert will have his little joke.

PHYLLIS. He's a duck.

WILL *returns by the main door.*

WILL. *(calling, up the stairs)* And put that light out, now! *(closing the door)* Getting that boy to sleep... Well, kids, got a drink?

PHYLLIS. Bill – *(suddenly ceremonious)* – a toast. *(raising her glass)* Long life to you an' Rona to enjoy the honour bestowed.

WILL. Thank you, Phyl. *(to **HAROLD**)* And how's the Blue Lion? Sit down! *(as **HAROLD** sits, in the arm-chair)* What news of the gang?

HAROLD. Cracker-jack. Couple o' casualties.

WILL. Oh?

HAROLD. Marjorie has to tickle the piano wi' one hand on account o' Reg havin' bashed her –

PHYLLIS. An' those two old bags from the West End got in wrong wi' the Navy –

HAROLD. The day after the party, an' you couldn't see 'em for dust –

WILL. *(laughing)*: I'd like to have been there for that! *(crossing to the fireplace)*

PHYLLIS. *(serious, suddenly)*: Oh, Harold...

HAROLD. Yes, honey?

PHYLLIS. What we come about. The party.

HAROLD. Oh yes... Bill, anything develop since?

WILL. *(putting coals on the fire)*: Since what?

PHYLLIS. Since we rung you up New Year's Day.

WILL. Did you?

PHYLLIS. *(to **HAROLD**)*: Albert never told him – so as not to worry him, what did I tell you –

WILL. *(turning to them)*: Why, what did you ring up about?

PHYLLIS. The party

WILL. What party?

PHYLLIS. A party you came and throwed at the Blue Lion, Christmas week-*your* party, you bad boy.

WILL. *(closing his eyes)*: Oh lord…

PHYLLIS. You've forgotten, I s'pose.

WILL. I'd like to forget the head I had the next morning, I know that…why, what happened?

HAROLD. *(to **WILL**)*: Well, New Year's morning, the bar in the Blue Lion opened early, for hangovers. We'd just been readin' in the paper –

PHYLLIS. *(to **WILL**)*: You know, about you turnin' into a knight –

HAROLD. When the chap next to us in the bar points to your picture on the front page. "You was at that party upstairs, wasn't you," he said, "the party this feller gave?" 'So what?' I said. And *he* said, "It was a dirty party, wasn't it?"

WILL. Oh.

PHYLLIS. *(to him)*: It was that rum we had, it's wicked stuff…

WILL. *(to **HAROLD**)*: What did you say?

HAROLD. "So what?" I said. "People took their clo'es off," he said, "and there was goin's on," he said. "So what?" I said, quick on the trigger.

PHYLLIS. *(to **WILL**)*: Somebody kept pullin' up the blind, I remember passin' a remark – an' the noise…

WILL. Mm… *(to **HAROLD**)* Did you tell him to mind his own business?

HAROLD. I did. "But it's public business," he said, "an' I've a good mind to go to the authorities," he said.

WILL. What did you do?

HAROLD. Gave him a drink an' told him to snap out of it.

WILL. Good for you –

HAROLD. But I didn't fancy the sound of it. Y'see, Bill, he give chapter an' verse.

WILL. Oh.

HAROLD. All about Phyl here wi' me an' Doreen –

WILL. *(chuckling)*: Oh oh oh – was your face red!

PHYLLIS. Don't…

HAROLD. An' so we thought better give you a tinkle –

PHYLLIS. A word o' warnin', sort o' thing –

WILL. Thank you, love, I appreciate it –

PHYLLIS. And we said to Albert on the phone for you to be sure and let us know everything was all right, an' when we didn't hear, you see, I thought to myself 'no news is bad news', and in the bar this mornin' when I seed your picture again in the *Mirror* and underneath about you goin' to be made official tomorrow, I said to Harold, we've got to see Bill tonight on our way to Maida Vale, I said, even if it means callin' at the house, I said.

HAROLD. *(to* **WILL***)*: Has anything happened since?

WILL. Not a thing.

HAROLD. *(rising, to* **PHYLLIS***)*: What did I tell you?

WILL. And it's over three months ago. Well, that's that.

PHYLLIS. Oh Bill, what a relief. Naughty Albert, isn't that nice… *(opening her bag and powdering her face, as* **HAROLD** *studies the bound volume on the desk)*

WILL. The moral being 'Pull the Blinds'.

PHYLLIS. You've made me blush, I was a naughty girl – *(smacking herself, on the arm)* – an' Harold, you ought to be ashamed o' yourself.

HAROLD. *(at the desk, holding up two volumes)*: Your books got lovely outsides, Bill.

WILL. *(smiling)* It's something, isn't it?

The **PARLOUR-MAID** *comes in by the main door.*

MAID. Excuse me, sir, it's Mr. Lampeter –

WILL. Good – *(as the* **MAID** *looks from* **PHYLLIS** *to* **HAROLD**, *puzzled)* – ask him in, out of the cold!

PHYLLIS. *(as the* **MAID** *goes out into the hall, to* **HAROLD**) She's wonderin' how we got in, oh dear…

WILL. *(in the main doorway, calling)* Thane? *(to the others)* I'd like you to meet an old friend of mine –

> **THANE** *comes in by the main door, taking off his overcoat; the* **MAID** *hovers in the doorway, holding his hat.*

– Thane, this is Phyllis – and this is Harold!

PHYLLIS. Pleased to meet you.

HAROLD. How d'ye do, sir?

THANE. *(after a pause, with a swift look from one to the other)* Good evening.

> *A pause, as* **THANE** *finishes getting out of his overcoat; the* **MAID** *steps forward and takes it.*

WILL. A drink, Thane?

THANE. No thank you, Will.

> *He sits, in the arm-chair; it is obvious that he has something on his mind. An awkward pause. The* **MAID** *turns to go out by the main door. The telephone rings. Involuntarily,* **PHYLLIS** *and* **HAROLD** *and* **WILL** *look at one another. The* **MAID** *answers the telephone.*

MAID. *(into the telephone)* This is Wellbeck 9732…

> **ALBERT** *hurries in by the kitchen door, and hurries forward.*

ALBERT. It's all right, I'll take it. *(taking the telephone from her, and speaking into it)* Sir William Trenting's house, yes?…*(as the* **MAID** *goes out by the main door, closing it behind her)* Who? *(to* **WILL**, *his hand over the mouthpiece)* A Mr. Bradby, sir.

THANE. Oh yes, he rang me this morning – it'll be about the profile he's writing of you on Sunday, in the *Observer.*

WILL. Oh. Thane, will you –

THANE. He's anxious to check one or two things, including your going to the Palace tomorrow – I think it'd be better if you spoke.

WILL. Oh. *(almost the sulky schoolboy)* All right…

PHYLLIS. To *Buckingham* Palace?

WILL. I'll take it in there, Albert –

> *He goes out by the main door, closing it behind him.*
> **ALBERT** *waits at the telephone.*

ALBERT. *(to* **THANE***)* Drink, sir?

THANE. Nothing for me, thank you, Albert.

HAROLD. *(to* **THANE***, looking at the telephone)* You weren't havin' us on just then – I mean about Bill goin' to Buckingham Palace?

THANE. No.

PHYLLIS. Isn't that nice…

WILL'S VOICE. *(through the telephone, in the drawing-room)*: Will Trenting speaking –

> **ALBERT** *replaces the receiver, looks from* **THANE** *to the other, and goes out by the kitchen door, closing it behind him.*

HAROLD. *(after a pause, to* **THANE***)*: Are you in the scribblin' racket?

THANE. I publish Mr. Trenting's books.

HAROLD. Mr Trenting – oh you mean *Bill!*

THANE. Bill?

HAROLD. We know him as Bill Trent, y'see –

PHYLLIS. *Mr.* Trenting? But aren't they Sir William an' Lady Trenting now?

THANE. Not officially, till tomorrow.

HAROLD. Oh I see…

PHYLLIS. *(after a pause)*: We're in the caterin' business. I'm behind the bar, my hubby travels.

THANE. Really.

PHYLLIS. *(on her best behaviour)*: I started on the stage. In my dad an' mum's repertory company, they was famous up north. I was a child actress, an' then I grew out of it.

THANE. Have you known 'Bill' long?

PHYLLIS. Couple of years on and off. He blows down to the Blue Lion for a long weekend, doesn't he, Harold, then we don't see him for six months at a time –

HAROLD. He's good value on a pub-crawl, is Bill… *(he goes to get himself another drink. A pause)* Terrible lot o' books, isn't there?

THANE. D'you read much?

HAROLD. It's the only thing that makes me feel sleepy.

THANE. Why is that?

HAROLD. They're all the same, aren't they?

THANE. Are they?

HAROLD. Well, I mean to say. They say a thing – an' then they say another. Then Chapter Two. Well, I mean to say!

> **WILL** *returns, and closes the main door.* **HAROLD** *is at the fireplace.*

THANE. All right?

WILL. A bit officious, but quite pleasant. Asked if tomorrow's the first time for me to wear a morning coat, and if it's taken Royalty to – *(mimicking)* – get me into one, doncherknow.

HAROLD. That's a good one –

THANE. Will, do you know anything about an indecent party in Rotherhithe?

> *A pause. The others stare at him.*

WILL. At a pub?

THANE. The Blue Lion.

WILL. *(as* **THANE** *looks from* **PHYLLIS** *to* **HAROLD***)* They know about it.

THANE. I know they do.

PHYLLIS. *(in a panic)* Oh no…

HAROLD. How d'you know?

THANE. From hearing your names mentioned, I'm afraid. Phyllis and Harold – Begham, is it?

PHYLLIS. Oh dear…

THANE. *(to* **WILL***)*: Did you give the party?

WILL. In my bed sitting-room. It was more a sort of impromptu booze-up, fifteen or twenty. People brought other people. *(ruefully)* Not your cup of tea, I'm afraid… But it was weeks ago! Who put you wise to all this?

THANE. The police.

A pause.

PHYLLIS. *(in a panic)* Oh dear… I knew there was something –

She stops abruptly, as **RONA** *comes in by the kitchen door, holding a glass of milk.* **THANE** *rises, nervously;* **PHYLLIS** *follows suit.*

RONA. Oh… I thought I heard somebody laughing just now – Thane dear, how nice – *(putting down the glass of milk, on the drinks table)* – do sit down, everybody –

WILL. Darling, this is Phyllis and Harold.

RONA. Oh?

WILL. You know –

RONA. *(going to shake hands with them, pleasantly, at the fireplace)*: Of course, Will's talked to me about you –

PHYLLIS. *(shyly)* I feel I know you, Ro – oh, hark at me bein' familiar mit Christian name –

RONA. *(as* **WILL** *pours himself a whisky)*: Don't be silly! Have you got drinks – Thane, won't you?

PHYLLIS *sits on the chair near* **RONA**'s *desk,* **RONA** *on the sofa.*

THANE. No thank you, my dear –

RONA. *(looking at him)*: Anything the matter?

THANE. No no –

RONA. *(amused)*: Thane, you look positively guilty!

WILL. I'm afraid he's arrived with a bit of bad news.

THANE. *(agitated)*: No, Will – I –

RONA. News? *(agitated)*: Ian… he's in bed… Will, what is it?

WILL. You know that party I told you about?

RONA. Rotherhithe? Yes?

WILL. The police have got on to it.

RONA. *(sharply)*: Oh no!

WILL. *(to* **THANE***)*: But how do you come into this?

THANE. *(hesitating, looking at* **RONA***)*: Well, I –

RONA. *(quickly)*: It's all right, Thane, please go on –

THANE. The thing was referred up to the headquarters today, to a C.I.D. man who's a member of the Savage, rather an admirer of your work. I just dined with him.

WILL finishes his drink, he is jolted.

HAROLD. But who told the police?

THANE. Some little man who suddenly got a bee in his bonnet –

HAROLD. *(to* **THANE***)*: But they can't run you in for bein' at a private party!

THANE. That's what the police told him, but he evidently made himself quite a nuisance.

WILL. But if it isn't a legal offence, why should they get on to you –

THANE. It's just that next time it might be that much uglier. It isn't so much a question of the law, as the press. For somebody in your position, it wouldn't look so pretty in the papers, would it? This fellow tonight wanted me to tip you off. Decent of him, I think. *(sitting, in the arm-chair)*

RONA. So they can't take any further steps this time?

THANE. No.

A general relief of tension. **WILL** *moves to the desk, then stops.*

WILL. *(on the defensive)*: By my position, you mean the knighthood.

THANE. It has helped.

WILL sits at the desk, angrily.

RONA. Well, it's a narrow escape. Thank God!… Like a drink, anybody?

PHYLLIS. *(to RONA)*: You're as sweet as Bill said you were… *(rising, immensely cheered, like a child)* Goody, goody, let's all have drinkies, shall we? *(to RONA)* D'you mind? *(pouring out, at the drinks table)*

HAROLD. *(looking at his watch, rising)*: Phyl, we ought to push off, we was due at ten. How far is Maida Vale?

PHYLLIS. Oh law, this has put me right off…

RONA. A party might cheer you up.

HAROLD. An' it's the first for weeks –

PHYLLIS. *(to RONA)*: Oh this isn't your sort of party. *(crossing to the desk and giving WILL his drink)*

RONA. I see. Oh dear… Is it the one Will told me about?

PHYLLIS. *(to WILL)*: Oh, you couldn't come now, dear, with your title and everything –

WILL. *(sharply, looking at THANE)*: Damn the title, I'm not going simply because I have to work!

He puts on his spectacles; RONA looks at him, quickly. ALBERT comes in by the kitchen door, carrying the hanger with the morning suit; he is now in his chauffeur's coat, his cap under his arm. WILL and PHYLLIS finish off their drinks.

ALBERT. Shall I put the car away, sir –

WILL. Drop them off first, will you?

PHYLLIS. Marv'lous – *(looking at ALBERT's uniform, as he hangs the hanger over the wardrobe cupboard)* – isn't he a smasher – home, James, an' don't spare the hosses –

The telephone rings. THANE rises and crosses to the fireplace.

ALBERT. *(into the telephone, suppressing a giggle)* Wellbeck 9732, Sir William Trenting's house…

WILL. *(finishing his drink, putting down his spectacles, and rising)*: We'll all have one first at the local shall we?

HAROLD. Good idea –

ALBERT. *(to **WILL**, covering the mouthpiece)* It's the B.B.C., sir.

WILL. Oh hell… Tell them I'm in bed.

RONA. They rang this afternoon –

THANE. It'll be about your speech at the luncheon tomorrow.

WILL. What's it got to do with them?

THANE. They're broadcasting it, and they want some idea of the length and what you're going to say, et cetera.

PHYLLIS. Oh, we mustn't miss that…

WILL. In other words, they want to censor it?

RONA. They just want a chat about it, I expect, you know what they are. *(crossing and taking **WILL**'s jacket)* Take it in the drawing-room, darling, so we don't disturb you – but put this on, it's cold in there –

PHYLLIS. *(to **WILL**)*: What a shame you can't have a drink –

WILL. *(going, pulling on his jacket)*: Bye-bye, you two –

HAROLD. So long, Bill, see you soon –

PHYLLIS. Bye-bye, love –

WILL. *(to them, looking at **THANE**)*: You have a good time.

He goes out by the main door, leaving it open, and to the left.

RONA *takes the telephone from **ALBERT**.*

RONA. *(into the telephone)*: He's just coming, so sorry…

THANE. *(quickly, as **ALBERT** makes to follow **WILL**)*: Albert, when you take them on to Maida Vale, don't drive right up to the address.

HAROLD. What's the idea?

THANE. The car might be watched, you never know.

HAROLD. I get you.

ALBERT. I could drop them at Maida Vale tube, sir –

HAROLD. Fine.

> **ALBERT** *goes out by the main door, to the right.*

WILL'S VOICE. *(through the telephone, in the drawing room)*: Will Trenting speaking.

> **RONA** *replaces the receiver.*

PHYLLIS. *(putting on her beret)*: Buckingham Palace, *well…*

RONA. Yes, and he's allowed two guests, isn't it exciting?

PHYLLIS. How lovely! Will you be nervous?

RONA. Very, but pleasantly so – it's not the same as if *I* were going to be presented.

PHYLLIS. D'you mean to say Bill'll be introduced, right close to?

RONA. As near as I am to you.

PHYLLIS. *Well…*

HAROLD. You know… *(thoughtfully)* … if I met the King, I wouldn't know what to say to him.

RONA. They make it awfully easy for you, you'd be surprised.

PHYLLIS. *You* haven't met them, have you?

RONA. Yes, I did once.

PHYLLIS. Oh, where?

RONA. At a garden party. I was so afraid I might fall over, I nearly did.

PHYLLIS. Well! *(rising, and turning to **THANE**, slightly ceremonious)* Au revoir. *(to **RONA**)* An' many congratulations on the honour bestowed.

HAROLD. Same here. *(bowing, slightly making fun of **PHYLLIS**)*

RONA. *(shaking hands with them)*: Thank you very much, both of you…*(as **HAROLD** and **PHYLLIS** move to go)* And for heaven's sake don't get into trouble.

PHYLLIS. *(a gesture of honest contrition)*: Oh dear…

HAROLD. No fear. *(in the main door, bowing deep to the room)* Honnie swah… *(taking **PHYLLIS** by the hand and going,* *doing his own version of the boogie-woogie)* Da-da-da, watch the window. Da-da-da, watch the window!

They go, to the right of the hall, **HAROLD** *closing the main door after them.* **RONA** *and* **THANE** *look at each other.*

THANE. I've known you both for fifteen years.

RONA. And you've found out more tonight than all the fifteen put together. *(taking up* **WILL***'s glass of milk, and sitting on the sofa)*

THANE. His books were obviously based on first-hand knowledge, but I delved no further.

RONA. You shut your eyes and published them?

THANE. *(smiling)*: *Touché…*

RONA. You see, Thane…*(thinking, carefully, earnestly)*… I'm not making excuses for Will, and I'd hate you to think I am, the thing's too important for that – but in fairness you have got to grant him one thing.

THANE. And what's that?

RONA. That this side of his life, which you're finding out about now – however unattractive you may think it is – does not come from the attitude of a writer in search of copy.

THANE. Oh, I don't question that – Will's work is obviously too good for anyone to think he's the type of novelist who goes slumming –

RONA. The thing about him is, that this side of his life springs inherently from his character as a *man*. He was like this before he ever put pen to paper, and he's stayed like it.

THANE. I see.

RONA. *(after a pause)*: Did you ever hear how I first met him?

THANE. At Lady Gott's, was it?

RONA. One of her literary dos – you know, the talk weaker than the drink… Suddenly, there was this shy well-behaved young man, answering my questions about poetry, in a way that would charm a bird off a tree. In the middle of those bleating hangers-on, his voice was forging words, he was alive… He left, I was taken on to Chelsea Arts Ball. I walked into a box thinking it was ours. There was the shy young man.

THANE. Drunk?

RONA. Too drunk to have locked the door.

THANE. Was he with a woman?

RONA. Two women. God knows where he'd picked them up. You can imagine how shocked I was. I sprang out as if I'd been shot. He rushed to the door.

THANE. To apologise?

RONA. Apologise? To ask me to join the party! I was dressed as Bo-Peep. I died with embarrassment. When I woke the next morning, the first thing that came into my mind, was opening that door.

THANE. And you thought 'Why didn't I knock?'

RONA. I thought "I'm going to marry that man" – isn't that awful?

THANE. Would many women have had that reaction?

RONA. Quite a few more, Professor, than would admit it… *(looking down at her glass of milk)* This ought to be a double brandy.

THANE. Then?

RONA. He asked me to marry him. At least he said – I remember exactly – 'Doctor Jekyll is anxious to marry you if you'll have him, but Mr Hyde insists on being at the wedding.'

THANE. So you knew you'd have to share him?

RONA. With Rotherhithe. The Chelsea Arts. Phyllis and Harold.

WILL *returns by the main door, leaving it open. He looks from one to the other, sensing that they have been discussing him.* RONA *finishes her milk.*

WILL. *(crossing to the desk)*: Did they get off all right?

RONA. Yes, darling – *(rising)*

WILL. Good.

There is a slight edge to his voice. He sits at the desk.

RONA. How was the B.B.C.?

WILL. Polite.

RONA. Difficult?

WILL. I'm afraid I was the difficult end. *(looking at* **THANE***)* I shall say what I like at the Lunch-ee-on, and I finished up by telling them so.

RONA. I'm afraid I've drunk your milk – I'll get into my dressing gown, then bring up another glass.

She goes out by the main door, closing it behind her. The two men are alone. **THANE** *is serious, thoughtful:* **WILL** *is self-conscious but calm, like a schoolboy caught in an embarrassing escapade. They look at each other.*

WILL. I'm sorry, Thane.

THANE. It takes a little adjusting to.

WILL. *(sharply)*: D'you think I've been a hypocrite?

THANE. NO, you've never pretended anything – everybody's always known where your sympathies lay. But there is a gap I have to bridge.

WILL. I see… What sort of gap, exactly?

THANE. Between seeing you as a sympathiser and realising you're an active participant. *(moving forward)* Quite a gap, after all these years.

WILL. The only person I had to be absolutely frank with was Rona. *(earnestly)* If you think I'd have enjoyed embarrassing my friends with my private life – I'm not exactly proud of it, you know—

THANE. Steady! … *(sitting in the arm-chair)* All I meant was that you've both been discreet, which is as it should be… But now that I know, I'm trying to fit it all together. A brothel over an East End pub, and the Nobel Prize. It isn't easy.

WILL. And yet if I'd never set foot in places like the Blue Lion, I wouldn't have written – Agnes in *The Deep Meadow;* so it's the brothel that got me the prize. And she's your favourite character.

THANE. I admire her as an artistic achievement –

WILL. But the real thing repels you?

THANE. Yes.

WILL. *(rising, eagerly)*: Now *that* I don't understand – with me the artistic achievement can take care of itself, what matters – surely – is the *real thing...* And *I'm* supposed to the literary man, not you!

THANE. *(thoughtfully)*: That may be the difference. You create, and I look on... Tell me more about the bed sitting-room.

WILL. Brown-paper peeling over half the window, faded pink forget-me-nots all over the wall, pictures of faded Highland cattle in among the forget-me-nots. *(as* **THANE** *looks round, unconsciously)* This room's important too, of course it is – but if I couldn't get away into the other I'd suffocate – can you understand that?... It isn't even that I stray as often as all that – until this damn weekend in December, I hadn't for a year.

THANE. And why then?

WILL. I'd just said yes to this Sir William business.

THANE. So you had to escape, into a dive where, any night, Bill Trent can collect a bunch of riff-raff and throw a 'party'. Or should I say 'orgy'?

WILL. *(ruefully)*: Orgy' does cover it, I'm afraid.

THANE. And it covers where those two are off tonight?

WILL. Definitely.

THANE. And you don't disapprove?

WILL. No. I can't see it's as bad as some things.

THANE. Such as?

WILL. Some of the films you see around. Posters with great luscious bosoms and underneath 'She Stopped at Nothing, Adults Only!' Think of the poor sex-starved bastard who pays his three bob and leans forward. What happens? Every time the two stars are kissing like blazes and about to grapple… fade-out, they're at breakfast. In the murk of Maida Vale, if Harold and Phyllis get the party spirit, there'll be no fade-out. You can't say it isn't honest.

THANE. Will they get paid?

WILL. I shouldn't be surprised.

THANE. Are they in need of the money?

WILL. Not strictly, he does odd jobs, she's behind the bar. But anything over's a great help… *(as* THANE *rises and walks to the fireplace)* That shocks you.

THANE. I'm afraid it does.

WILL. *(thoughtfully)*: And yet you are broad-minded… It doesn't shock me, isn't it funny? Those two'll be having a whale of a time- and what tickles me is that they'll quite likely spend the money on their little daughter's birthday, whom they love dearly. So are they worse that the parents who nag each other from twin beds by night, and are cruel to their children by day?

THANE. But your interest in this – you're not pretending it's healthy? *(sitting, on the sofa)*

WILL. Definitely sordid. Didn't you once say everybody has one vice? It looks like this is mine.

THANE. Go on.

WILL. Well, from the age of sixteen, I have been drawn towards promiscuous sex.

THANE. Towards loose women?

WILL. Women who will lean over in public and make an improper suggestion to men they've never met. And if the men look the women straight in the eye, wink and order drinks all round, my heart warms to the men. Rowdy, communal, unblushing… sex – I'm sorry but I'm fascinated by it. *(catching* THANE*'s eye)* Let's talk about existentialism.

He crosses to the desk, takes his empty glass, and goes to replenish it at the drinks table.

THANE. May I be cruder than you?

WILL. Crude as you like.

THANE. Do you sleep with these women?

WILL. *(after a pause)*: Sometimes.

THANE. Did it happen at this… party?

WILL. Yes.

THANE. A woman you knew?

WILL. No. She came over to my corner. I was pretty drunk, and I lost interest. I can give you any details I remember, but are they necessary?

THANE. You lost interest?

WILL. *(thoughtfully)*: Actually that has never been so important. It does happen, of course, but it happens the way it did that night – pretty well by chance.

THANE. You mean the society of these individuals is what matters to you?

WILL. *(eagerly)*: That's it! I suppose I'm attracted by people who are – disreputable.

THANE. You mean vicious?

WILL. Sordid, raw, impudent… vicious. If they're on the plump side, and have a native wit, and have never heard of my books, I like them even more.

THANE. And when she sits on the edge of a rumpled bed scratching her scalp –

WILL. I like her more than ever. There's one called Dorrie Morton – you've just described her. She and her pal Madge, a bit older, both in hair curlers –

THANE. *(rising, and walking to the fireplace)*: I'm sorry, but when it isn't distasteful it sounds ridiculous –

WILL. Of course it's ridiculous, but that's what I like too! *(sitting on the sofa end)* I remember Dorrie one morning, sitting on the bed – nothing on – having a Guinness with me and Madge, and telling us about her mother's death. She was looking out of the window, past the brown paper. She started to cry. A tear rolled down her big cheek and plopped on to her breast. The hand round the Guinness had the little finger crooked as if it held a very thin tea cup. That great unconscious face, those stupid beautiful eyes… The day before, I'd been trapped into one of those literary lunches; looking at her I thought about those voices droning on about life at second-hand, and I thought 'Dorrie my girl, you make them look like well bred rubbish'. I feel at home with Dorrie, and Harold, and Phyllis. They're no good, but they're the real thing. I love them.

He rises and crosses to the desk.

THANE. Doesn't Dorrie take money, too?

WILL. Some black-market fellow from the docks once gave her a fiver; she raised hell till it had another next to it for company. But there isn't anything wicked about her! She's sordid, *and* ridiculous. *(leaning forward, with a mixture of cruelty and affection)* The same bunch of human beings, half-drunk and half-naked in a half-light against pink forget-me-nots and Highland cattle, can look comic enough for any cartoonist; but it doesn't prevent it from being tremendously… alive.

A pause.

THANE. *(turning abruptly)*: I'll say good-night.

WILL. You asked for it. Good-night.

He sits again at his desk, to work. THANE *moves towards the main door, stops and turns.*

THANE. Do you believe that the life you lead is right?

WILL *looks up. A pause.*

WILL. *(carefully)*: I believe that the life I lead is right, for me. If it harms anybody, it'll harm me.

RONA *comes in by the kitchen door; she is in her dressing gown, and carries another glass of milk.*

RONA. What have you been arguing about, Henry James? Don't go, Thane – *(looking at the clock)* – you're just in time for the broadcast.

THANE. *(looking at his watch)*: Yes, of course –

RONA. *(switching on the portable radio, then crossing to* **WILL***)*: Your milk, darling.

WILL. *(drinking)* Thank you, dear, but I'm being a devil on whisky.

> **RONA** *looks at him, then at* **THANE.** *Piano music, on the radio.* **RONA** *looks to see where to put the glass of milk,* **THANE** *puts out a hand for it; she gives it to him, then takes a copy of the* Radio Times *from next to the radio, sits on the stool, and studies it.* **THANE**'s *eyes go from* **WILL** *to her, and back again.* **WILL** *feels* **THANE**'s *eyes on him.*

Thane, d'you *mean* to look as if you were studying something in the Zoo?

THANE. *(confused)*: Sorry.

> **WILL** *tries to go back to his work. The music finishes, on the radio.* **RONA** *sits on the stool, to listen.*

ANNOUNCER'S VOICE. *(on the radio, a typical conventional B.B.C. product)* This is the B.B.C. Home Service. This evening, in our series 'Talks on Famous Writers', Professor Paul Risdon will be speaking on 'Will Trenting, Romantic Realist'. Professor Risdon.

PROFESSOR'S VOICE. *(on the radio, pleasant, but again intensely conventional)* Will Trenting – a name more familiar to the public than 'Sir William', his official designation from now on – *(as* **WILL** *rises, and crosses abruptly to the radio)* – is probably the most challenging figure in European lit –

> **WILL** *switches off the radio.*

RONA. *(looking up, startled)*: Darling, no –

WILL. *(striding back to the desk)*: You don't want to hear a lot of pompous clichés about –

RONA. I do, he's a very good man—

WILL. We'll give a dinner, shall we? White tie and tails, and he can sing at the piano.

He sits back at this desk and turns pages. RONA *controls her annoyance, and looks at him. He catches her look, sharply.* Anything the matter?

RONA. I was wondering if you should have had your hair cut, but it looks all right.

WILL. What for?

RONA. Tomorrow morning, Buckingham Palace. *(as* WILL *goes back to his papers)* I know it's bourgeois to keep appointments.

WILL. *(looking at her like a mutinous child)* Do I have to go to The Savoy after?

RONA. *(loosing patience, rising)*: It's a luncheon *for* you, eighty people. I don't care if I do sound like your mother, *please* try to be –

WILL. *(rising, and walking)*: Did I ask them?

THANE. *(rising, embarrassed)*: I think I'll be getting along –

RONA. It's raining, Albert'll take you –

WILL. Have you any idea what a damn fool I looked in that hire-clothes place, trying on that coat, without any trousers on.

RONA. *(exasperated)*: But you'll have your trousers on in Buckingham Palace! Oh, what nonsense we're talking –

WILL. *(to* THANE*)*: Do they ever take titles back?

RONA. *(in a level voice)* I should think it's like shops, dear, once you've soiled something, it's not returnable.

WILL. Thank you. *(he sits back at the desk.* RONA *turns to* THANE*)* So I'm childish, am I?

RONA. I didn't say anything.

A pause. WILL *crumples up the page of manuscript in front of him, throws it into the waste-paper basket, rises, opens the door of the cupboard, and puts on an old raincoat.*

Are you going out?

WILL. I'm going for a walk.

RONA. It's pouring – must you?

WILL. I've been cooped up in here all day –

RONA. Would you like to go to the party?

THANE. *(startled)*: The party?

RONA. Marian's got a few people in… *(smiling)* Thane, you thought I meant the other party, how awful-no, that would not have been a good idea… Will, what about Marian?

WILL. I don't feel like making conversation about the trend of the novel. Sorry… *(walking down to her, slowly)* What did you mean, about the other party?

RONA. What did I say?

WILL. That I'm not allowed to go to it.

RONA. Of course you're *allowed* to go to it – but I don't think it'd be a very attractive gesture, the night before you get your knighthood, however little you may think of it –

WILL. There! Now we have it. You've said it!

RONA. Said what?

WILL. *(a little drunk by now)*: I have now *got* to behave myself. *(mimicking)* Sir William, you can't go here, you can't be seen there –

RONA. *(at the end of her tether)*: If you won't face the fact that you're skating on thin ice, then nothing will make you, I do know that… Go for your walk, get nice and wet, and then to bed with a chill, and I promise not to say 'I told you so'. Sorry to answer back, but I can lose my temper too.

WILL. *(after a pause)*: What bus would get me across to Maida Vale, d'you think?

They look at him.

THANE. You're joking.

WILL. I've been asked to a party and I'm going to it. Sorry.

He moves to go; **RONA** *goes to him.*

RONA. *(appealing to him)*: Will… You don't even *want* to go, do you?

WILL. Don't I?

RONA. It's nice and warm in here, and you know perfectly well there'll be people there who'll bore you as much as anybody would at Marian's – that last party in Rotherhithe, you went to sleep half-way through, you told me –

WILL. *(with obstinate infuriating calm)*: I'm a grown man who's been asked to a private party in a free country. Sorry.

He goes out by the main door and into the hall. The sound of the front door banging, **RONA** *and* **THANE** *look at each other.*

RONA. I can hear myself sounding like his mother, but can I stop? … *(vehemently) Damn* the knighthood… Well, Phyllis and Harold have won this time. And I'm for bed.

THANE. Are you jealous?

RONA. No.

THANE. Why not?

RONA. Because although he wouldn't admit it – certainly not in this mood – Ian and I are more important to him than all the others put together. Good-night, my dear –

THANE. So all's right with the world?

RONA. *(looking at him)*: No. Not quite all right.

THANE. Will thinks so.

RONA. It's no good pretending I don't wish he were – otherwise… But if he were, how do we know he'd still have talent? And he might not even be human, in which case I wouldn't have wanted a thing to do with him – so where are you?

THANE. And you've compromised?

The telephone rings.

RONA. *(going to it)*: I've compromised... *(with a sigh)* And I hope the result isn't too bad... *(into the telephone, after a pause)* He's out, I'm afraid... Yes, *he's* here. *(to* THANE, *her hand over the mouthpiece)* Wants you, rather mysterious –

THANE. Me?

RONA. *(as he comes to her)*: Don't tell me you're leading a double life –

THANE. *(into the telephone)*: Hello... Oh... I don't think so...

ALBERT *enters by the main door; he carries his chauffeur's cap.* RONA *is watching* THANE.

ALBERT. Anything more tonight, my lady?

THANE. *(into the telephone)*: Thank you, good-night... *(he hangs up, perturbed)*

RONA. *(to him)* Who was that?

THANE. The man I dined with tonight.

RONA. The – Scotland Yard man?

THANE. The police had phoned him, since.

RONA. Why?

THANE. About the party tonight. They'd heard Will had been asked to it.

RONA. But why –

THANE. It's going to be raided.

A pause.

RONA. He's probably gone by bus. Drive straight back to the address, Albert, and catch him before he goes in.

ALBERT. I dropped the two of 'em off at Maida Vale tube – *(to* THANE*)* – like you suggested, sir.

RONA. *(to* THANE, *desperately)*: Ring him back – get him to stop the raid –

THANE. I'm afraid he'd say it's now out of his hands... *(to* **ALBERT***)* You have no idea where the house is?

ALBERT. No, sir. Sorry.

A pause.

RONA. His address book–

ALBERT. He's got it on him, my lady... I could cruise up an' down the district –

RONA. On the chance – do, **ALBERT** – hurry!...

> **ALBERT** *runs out into the hall.* **THANE** *and* **RONA** *look at each other. The curtain falls, and rises immediately on*

Scene Three

> *The next morning. The curtains are closed; the light through them is grey and wintry.* **THANE** *sits in the armchair reading* **WILL***'s press-cutting book (now completed), in stockinged feet and wearing* **WILL***'s dressing-gown. His own coat is over a chair. On the sofa,* **RONA** *sits dozing against a pillow; she is still in her dressing-gown. The typing table is now against the bookshelves next to the wardrobe cupboard, and remains there for the rest of the play: its chair stays in front of the desk.*

RONA. I thought I heard the door.

THANE. It was the maid, I think.

> **ALBERT** *comes in from the kitchen, carrying two cups of tea on a tray. He is in shirt-sleeves, and wears a carpenter's apron. (taking a cup)* Oh thank you Albert.

ALBERT. *(looking at the windows)*: Shall I –

RONA. Yes, open them, will you, Albert?

> **ALBERT** *opens the curtains: watery morning light outside.* **IAN** *hurries in by the main door. He is in his shirtsleeves, and looks worried.*

IAN. Mummy, your bed hasn't been slept in! *(seeing the pillow)* Where's Dad? Is he in hospital?

RONA. No, darling, he was – away for the night –

ALBERT. At his Auntie Meg's in St. Albans, she's bad again.

IAN. Oh… *(worried)* If she dies, will he be very upset?

RONA. Sad but not upset, she is ninety-four. *(drinking tea)*

IAN. Ninety-*four*?… *(going)* He's lucky she's still alive.

> *He goes out by the main door, leaving it open, and goes upstairs.*

RONA. Thank you, Albert. I think the old lady'd forgive us.

> **ALBERT** *smiles, and goes towards the kitchen;* **RONA** *and* **THANE** *drink their tea. A sharp rat-tat-tat at the front door;* **RONA** *and* **THANE** *look at each other, then at* **ALBERT**. **ALBERT** *goes out by the main door and into the hall.* **THANE** *rises, leaving the press cutting book on the sofa.* **ALBERT** *returns, and holds out a telegram to* **RONA**. *She looks from him to* **THANE**, *braces herself, tears open the envelope, and reads the telegram.*

> *(reading)* "Congratulations, The Pen Club".

> *She looks from* **THANE** *to* **ALBERT**; *they relax.*

All right, Albert, no answer.

> **ALBERT** *goes out by the main door, closing it behind him.* **RONA** *crosses to the desk and lays the telegram opposite* **WILL***'s chair. The false alarm has shaken her.*

It's rather cold, but I think I'll open a window – *(flinging one window open, with an urgent gesture.)*

THANE. What sort of morning is it?

RONA. It's been raining, and you can smell the park. Fresh like the country –

> *She cries, suddenly, unexpectedly.* **THANE** *takes a step to her.*

Don't move, Thane, I'm all right, just tired… *(turning, and seeing his face)* Thane… for his sake and mine, should I have said 'No, I won't take you on those terms'?

They look at each other, **ALBERT** *comes in by the main door; he stands to one side. He is hiding his pleased excitement.*

ALBERT. *(announcing, formally)* Mr. and Mrs. Begham.

RONA. Begham? *(confused)* But Albert, who are they, I can't see anybody –

ALBERT *is followed, from the hall, by* **HAROLD** *and* **PHYLLIS**. *They are in the same clothes as the night before, but look scruffier.*

RONA. Phyllis!

PHYLLIS. Christmas, what a night…

RONA. *(urgently)*: *Was* it raided?

HAROLD. Raided?

PHYLLIS. Why, was it going to be?

RONA. Didn't you go? Didn't Will go?

PHYLLIS. No.

RONA *looks from* **THANE** *to* **ALBERT***, and breathes a sigh of relief.* **ALBERT** *goes to the desk to sort the morning mail. Listening in the meantime.*

Harold and me got there late, we'd had a drink with Albert, then the walk to the house… Well, at the gate something came o'er me. I couldn't budge, not to save me life. My mother was psychic, you see. Isn't that weird?

HAROLD. *(to the others):* It was Albert here scared us.

PHYLLIS. He was in the police once, he told us, and the tales! Well, just as I heard this psychic voice, up the street walks Bill.

RONA. Bill – oh yes, Will …

PHYLLIS. I refused to stir inside the gate, he got quite sarcastic.

HAROLD. "All right" he said, "where'd you two killjoys like to go, the Four Hundred?"

THANE. What did you say?

PHYLLIS. I said 'yes'.

HAROLD. And we went.

ALBERT helps THANE *to change from dressing-gown and stockinged feet to his own coat and shoes.*

RONA. *(sitting back, laughing with relief)*: Oh dear... Albert, I didn't know you'd ever been in the police force?

PHYLLIS. *(as* ALBERT *smiles)*: Albert!

ALBERT closes the window and hangs up the dressing gown in the cupboard; HAROLD *crosses to the fireplace.*

RONA. *(to* PHYLLIS *and* HAROLD*)*: But you have to be dressed for the Four Hundred!

HAROLD. Bill slipped 'em something for a table behind a curtain –

PHYLLIS. And I was near the cream-de-la-cream as I am to you.

HAROLD. I'd never ha' guessed the evening'd end like that

RONA. *(a great weight off her mind)*: Now breakfast, you must be famished –

HAROLD. Oh, that's all right –

RONA. No, doesn't matter a bit – Albert, tell Mrs. Preston, spin her a yarn, you'll know how –

ALBERT nods reassuringly and goes out by the kitchen door. PHYLLIS *takes her coat off and places it on the sofa.*

How long did you stay at the Four Hundred?

PHYLLIS. Till closin' time. Then Bill bought champagne for the band an' the waiters, an' we danced. I was droppin' but the bubbly picked my feet up. Then we went to Covent Garden Market and had drinkies wi' some porters, an' we was there till now. An' then he *would* put us in a taxi to come here for breakfast –

HAROLD. And if no answer here, to go to Number Ten Blenheim Gardens and ask for the Purity League.

THANE. *My* address.

HAROLD. The last we saw of him was sittin' on the Embankment.

PHYLLIS. Watching the river. Isn't he weird?

RONA. Ah well… *(kissing* THANE, *as* PHYLLIS*'s eye catches the framed photograph on* RONA*'s desk)* Thank you, my dear, for everything. *(to the others, going towards the main door)* I'll see you in a minute –

PHYLLIS. *(holding the photograph)*: What a lovely baby – how much did he weigh?

RONA. Seven pounds. You've got a little girl, haven't you?

PHYLLIS. Brenda.

HAROLD. She tipped the scales at eight.

RONA. *(looking at the snapshot which* HAROLD *has automatically produced from his wallet)*: She's like her father isn't she?

HAROLD. *(slapping his chest, at* THANE*)*: Ah ha!

> RONA *smiles, and hurries out by the main door, and upstairs.*

PHYLLIS. Isn't she nice?

HAROLD. Smasher –

THANE. I think I'll get home and take a bath.

PHYLLIS. I hope you enjoy the lunch.

THANE. Thank you.

PHYLLIS. *(as he goes)*: Cheer-ho for now.

THANE. *(pleasant, but constrained)*: Good-bye.

HAROLD. Be good.

> THANE *goes into the hall, closing the main door behind him.*

PHYLLIS. *(sitting on the sofa)*: Poor chap, he don't get much of a run for his money, does he? … *(her head against the pillow)* Ooh, I'm tired, but that bandleader was a smashin' crooner… *(waltzing around haphazard)* Next time I hear him on the wireless, I'll think – *(crooning)* – 'I've danced with you.'

HAROLD. *(crooning)*: 'And you're five foot two'

PHYLLIS. He told me he'd bought a villa for four thousand.

HAROLD. Why didn't you ask him to show you over it?

PHYLLIS. I'd just informed him I had my hubby with me.

HAROLD. *(good humouredly)*: That's a damn silly thing to give away when we have a night out, isn't it.

PHYLLIS. I love his voice, but I went right off him while we was dancin', isn't that funny...

HAROLD. That's different... Bill weren't himself last night, did you notice?

PHYLLIS. You're in the middle of tellin' him something, an' he's miles away.

HAROLD. It's all that writin'. *(sitting on the desk)*

PHYLLIS. Ooh, that other scare about the police, an' now this raid... Harold, d'you think we ought to give it up?

HAROLD. Give what up?

PHYLLIS. It.

HAROLD. Business plus pleasure, what's wrong with it?

PHYLLIS. *(sitting in the arm-chair)*: It was rainin' Tuesday, and I sheltered in the Salvation Army on my way to the Lion. The organ was carryin' on regardless, and I got thinkin' about things Mum told me, and I was sniffin' so, they had to come up to see what was cookin'. Then it stopped rainin' and I went an' had a gin, and I felt better... It's breakfast time, and d'you know what I'd like to do, *now*?

HAROLD. What?

PHYLLIS. Go to a dance.

The main door opens and **IAN** *enters, carrying a book. He is in his best clothes. He shuts the door;* **HAROLD** *and* **PHYLLIS** *watch him. He makes to go to the bookcase.*

You're Ian, aren't you?

IAN. *(turning)*: Yes.

PHYLLIS. Are you goin' to Buckingham Palace?

IAN. Yes.

PHYLLIS. D'you like reading?

IAN. Very much. What do *you* think of Dickens?

PHYLLIS. He's a good author, isn't he?

HAROLD. *(to her)*: Careful, ducks...

IAN. *(to* **PHYLLIS***)*: Which do *you* like best?

HAROLD. Careful…

PHYLLIS. *(after a pause)*: *The Old Curiosity Shop.*

IAN. I didn't like the end, did you?

PHYLLIS. No, I didn't.

IAN. How do you think it should have ended?

> **HAROLD** *covers his eyes.*

PHYLLIS. *(without hesitation)*: Wi' Quilp the dwarf dying an' Nell an' her dad happy ever after.

IAN. *(as* **HAROLD** *stares)*: You mean the old man *shouldn't* have died?

PHYLLIS. No he shouldn't, he was a duck.

HAROLD. *(to her)*: How *d'you* know?

PHYLLIS. I played Nell, wi' Mum as the Marchioness.

IAN. *(eyes wide)*: You were *Little Nell*?

PHYLLIS. I was younger then, thirteen.

IAN. *(fascinated)*: Gosh… Did you have to say 'I have had a dreadful dream. It is a dream – '

PHYLLIS. *(in a matter-of-fact voice as if she played the part last night)*: A dream of grey-haired men, in darkened rooms by night, robbin' sleepers of their gold.'

IAN. Gosh!

> **RONA** *comes in by the main door, leaving it open; she has changed into her dress for the morning, and is ready except for final touches.*

RONA. Breakfast's in.

HAROLD and **PHYLLIS**. Thank you.

IAN. Mummy, she's been Little Nell!

RONA. *(hardly listening)*: How nice – *(to the others)* – I'll be along in a second –

IAN. Mummy, can I sit with them? *(to* **PHYLLIS** *eagerly)* Can you remember any of the other scenes?

PHYLLIS. I'll try – *(picking up her coat and handbag.)*

RONA. You *played* in it? But how wonderful! He'll never give you a minute's peace –

IAN. *(going out by the main door, to* **PHYLLIS***)*: Did you die in the last scene?

PHYLLIS. Till the inspectors came round, and then wi' the cruelty to children I had to die an hour and a 'alf earlier...

They disappear to the left, talking animatedly. **HAROLD** *looks at* **RONA** *and follows them.* **RONA**, *alone, gives a sigh of relief, looks at her watch, then makes up her lips in the mirror.*

The sound of the front door closing; she stops, listens, then goes on with what she was doing. **WILL** *enters by the main door, from the hall. He wears his raincoat, looks tired and unkempt, but has (unexpectedly) an air of abstracted calm. He sees* **RONA**.

RONA. Good morning.

WILL. *(after a second, sheepishly)*: Good morning...

He crosses to the desk, and picks up the sheets of manuscript on which he was working last evening; he looks a **RONA**.

Darling, it's coming right.

RONA. What?

WILL. That third chapter. It suddenly came to me, sitting on the Embankment. *(crossing, to* **RONA***)* I'd been seeing it complicated – it *must* be simple. The mother's home from jail, opens the door, the child's face tells everything –

RONA. You mean make the *child* pretend?

WILL. That's it. The *mother's* the ingenuous one, not the child! It'll make all the difference, won't it.

RONA. You won't tamper with the scenes outside the house?

WILL. No no, the soldier still meets her coming home, only now it's already dawn, d'you see? She's in that ludicrous evening dress, but somehow transfigured –

RONA. Because the child's pretended – *(excited)* – oh *yes!* It's different, and yet it's true- I am glad…

WILL. *(seeing the pillow, on the sofa)*: What's that doing down here?

RONA. Thane and I sat up.

WILL. But why?

RONA. The police rang to say the party was going to be raided.

WILL. *(startled)*: Raided?

The main door opens, **IAN**'s *head comes round it; he is eating a piece of toast.*

IAN. Is Dad – *(seeing* **WILL***)* – I told Phyllis I heard the door! *(to* **WILL***)* Is your Auntie Meg dead yet?

WILL. Dead?

RONA. *(to him, quickly)*: You had to go her in the night, you remember – *(to* **IAN** *)*—she's better.

IAN. Oh. I thought perhaps she was dead.

He goes out again by the main door, closing it behind him. **WILL** *and* **RONA** *look at each other.*

WILL. And you thought I'd gone to it… Did you get *any* sleep?

RONA. Don't you think a move-on? You've got a date.

WILL breaks down and sits, clasping her round the knees.

WILL. My darling, my darling… what makes me like this… I'm sorry, I'm sorry… What's driving me?

RONA. Just yourself my love. And you're quite a driver.

He rises; they kiss warmly. **RONA** *looks at the clock.*

WILL. I'll get ready.

He takes the pillow, crosses, takes down the hanger with the morning suit, looks at it sheepishly, and goes out by the main door and upstairs. **RONA** *sighs, as she would after a hopeless child, and tidies cushions.* **ALBERT** *comes in from the hall, looking uncertainly up the stairs as he passes them.*

ALBERT. Excuse me, my lady – it's a Mr. Daker.

RONA. Daker? Conveys nothing to me.

ALBERT. He's from Rotherhithe, my lady.

RONA. Rotherhithe?

> *From the hall* **DAKER** *comes into the room past* **ALBERT***, with a shuffling diffident movement, hat in hand.*

DAKER. Lady Trenting? My name is Daker.

> *He is a small insignificant man of fifty, shabby-genteel. He shows as yet no signs of menace; his manner is polite, with a touch of affable subservience. He speaks well, if too precisely. His delivery tends to be quick and nervous.*
>
> **ALBERT** *tidies the desk, one eye on the visitor.*

RONA. *(pleasantly)* What did you want to see us about?

DAKER. It's rather difficult – *(looking out of the window)* – the lawn and the spire, quite perfect, and it's dirty old London – you know what it reminds me of, Lady Trenting? Cambridge. That bit of the backs - oh dear, I find it affecting.

RONA. *(taking the hint)*: You were at Cambridge?

DAKER. *(with a deprecating laugh)*: Let's not go into that… And what a pleasant room, do I detect the feminine touch? *(seeing the picture below the window)* Utrillo?

RONA. It's a Bonnard

DAKER. Oh I could have sworn a Utrillo –

> *He moves over to the picture, stops, sways slightly for a second, and moves on.* **RONA** *looks at* **ALBERT***, who makes the quick gesture of putting a glass to his mouth; they (and the audience) realise for the first time that* **DAKER** *is a drunkard.* **ALBERT** *goes back into the hall, closing the main door.*

> Of course it's a Bonnard, *quelle gaffe,* such composition –

RONA. Do you live in Rotherhithe?

DAKER. For my sins …*(crossing, to* **RONA***)* Lady Trenting, what a wealth of comment in that quiet little question – 'do you live in Rotherhithe'!

RONA. *(taken aback)*: I'm so sorry

DAKER. Not at all, you did it beautifully…

His voice dies away as he examines the picture over the mantelpiece.

WILL *bursts in by the main door; he is wearing his striped trousers, is in shirt-sleeves and black waistcoat. He crosses to the wardrobe cupboard.*

WILL. Darling, you haven't seen the collar and tie for this outfit, have you?

Opening the cupboard door.

RONA. Will, here's somebody you know.

WILL. *(turning)*: I'm so sorry… *(seeing* DAKER*)* Oh. Good morning.

DAKER. *(coming forward, past* RONA*)*: How do you do, Sir William, I don't think we've met.

WILL. No I don't think so. *(going back to the cupboard)* Excuse me, I have an appointment- oh yes, here they are… *(taking a collar and tie from a shelf, and fixing them on.)*

DAKER. So my paper told me yesterday, very exciting…

RONA. Mr. Daker's from Rotherhithe.

WILL. *(after a pause)*: Oh?

RONA. You haven't an awful lot of time, darling… Shall I send something in – Mr. Daker, tea or coffee?

DAKER. Choice of tea or coffee, can I believe these old ears, coffee would be spiffing…

He is examining the bound edition. RONA *looks at* WILL, *and goes out by the kitchen door, closing it behind her.* DAKER *and* WILL *are alone.* WILL *ties his tie quickly.*

The works of Will Trenting… As an author myself I can imagine the joy of seeing one's work in print…

WILL. You're an author?

DAKER. In my tiny way, spare my blushes.

WILL. Have you written much?

DAKER. *(after a pause)*: Quite an amount. But I've not been lucky, I – *(his hand to his chest)* – do forgive me, I feared rain, and quickened my pace across the park...

WILL. I'm so sorry – a drop of brandy? *(one foot on the arm of the arm-chair, fastening a shoe-lace)* It's there – *(as* **DAKER** *crosses to the drinks table)* – should be the middle decanter.

DAKER. Very kind of you, it might steady this fluttering – *(pouring a brandy)* – how very kind of you.

WILL. *(turning and facing* **DAKER** *after the latter has taken a gulp)* Well, what is it?

DAKER. Rather a painful – er – I hardly know...

WILL. Let me help you. Is it to do with the Blue Lion?

DAKER. The public house where you – er – go in search of copy, indeed yes... *(clerically waggish, sitting on the sofa)* Bohemia, Bohemia, what naughty deeds come to light in thy name...

WILL. I must ask you to get to the point. What is the exact–

DAKER. *(Suddenly, affably)*: The twenty-second of December.

WILL. Twenty-second... Sorry, offhand that conveys nothing.

DAKER. The night of your party at the Blue Lion.

WILL. *(after a pause)*: Oh. So you were the Peeping Tom who went to the police –

DAKER. The night you had your camera and – click, click... *(making the gesture of taking a snapshot, and laughing, like a sly nervous uncle)*...ha ha...

WILL. A camera? What d'you mean, a camera?

DAKER. The indecent photographs.

A pause.

WILL. Indecent ph...what are you talking about? What photographs?

DAKER *takes a small grubby sealed envelope from his breast pocket.*

DAKER. Spare my blushes – not for Aunt Agatha, eh? Ha ha –

WILL. But this is the first I've heard – it must have been after I passed out –

DAKER. No doubt, no doubt. Unfortunate that it should have been your camera.

WILL. I haven't got a camera.

DAKER. It has your name, on a tag.

WILL. So that's what happened to it – it was pinched! It was a Christmas present, for my little boy, I'd bought it on the way there... How did *you* get hold of it?

DAKER. I was in the café last week where the pictures were being offered for sale. (*putting the envelope back in his pocket*)

WILL. Oh.

DAKER. (*leaning over and studying the press-cutting book, which is beside him*):

Mind you, I said nothing to the police about them... Your press-cuttings, Sir William? A fascinating array...

ALBERT's knock at the main door; he enters, carrying WILL's morning coat, comes down to WILL, and holds out the coat. WILL takes it; ALBERT goes back, closing the main door behind him.

WILL. Well the whole thing's made me feel damn silly – which I deserve – but I've been lucky. I (*putting on the coat*) As you must know, the authorities were pretty good about it–

DAKER. (*helping him on with the coat*): Isn't that a blessing, Sir William, did you have to pay much?

WILL. (*coldly*): Oddly enough no... (*going to the cupboard*) You'll be relieved to hear that the subject is closed. (*shutting the cupboard doors, then going to the window*) I don't think it's started to rain –

DAKER. But the subject is not closed.

He sits again on the sofa. WILL looks at him.

WILL. How do you mean?

DAKER. Among your guests at your – er – party… do you recall a girl named Joan?

WILL. Joan – with a sailor? A big girl?

DAKER. Rather *petite*, with a fox fur.

WILL. With her hair up on top?

DAKER. That's the one. You recall her now?

WILL. *(after a pause)*: I didn't know her, she was brought by somebody.

DAKER. But during the evening, in a corner of the room, you became acquainted?

WILL. Yes.

DAKER. You even – how shall I word it – got to know her rather well.

WILL. *(angrily)*: May I ask what business that is of yours?

DAKER. How old would you have said she was?

WILL. Oh. Twenty-four? Five?

DAKER. What difference these hair styles can make, and of course her escort had borrowed the fur for her –

WILL. Why, how old *is* she?

DAKER. She will be fifteen next month.

A pause.

WILL. Do you expect me to believe you?

DAKER . I'm afraid you have no alternative.

WILL stares at him.

WILL. You're her father?

DAKER. I am.

IAN enters from the main door, eagerly. WILL stares at DAKER.

IAN. *(crossing to a bookshelf and climbing the library steps)*: I just want to show Phyllis something…

He takes a book and hurries out, closing the main door behind him, as the curtain falls.

INTERVAL

Scene Four

Immediately afterwards. **WILL** *is staring at* **DAKER***;*
DAKER *is looking at the main door, which has just closed
after* **IAN***.* **DAKER** *turns again to* **WILL***.*

WILL. What proof have you of this?

DAKER. *(fumbling in his breast pocket)*: I have here Joanie's
birth certificate. *(holding it out)* April the eleventh,
nineteen thirty-six. *(putting it back)* And it needs no
great feat of arithmetic, Sir William, to prove that if
she was born on April the eleventh, nineteen thirty six,
my daughter *will* be fifteen next month.

WILL. *(deeply shocked)*: I'd never have let her in, not in a
thousand years... I had no idea, she behaved like a
very experienced woman –

THE **PARLOUR-MAID** *enters by the kitchen door, carrying
a tray with a cup of coffee.*

DAKER. And you know the law of the land about procuring –

He sees the **MAID***, and stops short. She brings him the
cup of coffee.* **WILL***, as if stunned, walks slowly round
the foot of the desk, and sits at it.*

(taking the cup): How very kind of you...

He watches the **MAID***, out of the corner of his eye, till she
has gone back by the kitchen door and closed it behind
her.*

And you know the law of the land, about procuring
children? *(as* **WILL** *stares at him)* It's very sad. There
are just the two of us, Joanie and me. *(rising, putting
the untouched cup of coffee down on the drinks table, and
wending his way across the room towards* **WILL***)*

A horrible suspicion had crossed my mind, after she
went out that evening, that she was being taken to your
party.

I posted myself on the other side of the road and
kept watch, until the cold weather proved too much

for me – so you'll admit, Sir William, that when you labelled me a 'Peeping Tom', you were not being *quite* fair... But I failed to see her – mercifully perhaps. For weeks I thought no more, until Saturday night, in the café, when an even more horrible suspicion occurred to me that one of the – er – pornographic pictures included a young person not unlike my Joanie.

WILL. *(deeply perturbed)*: Oh God –

DAKER. I taxed her with it. She broke down and confessed.

He sits in ALBERT*'s typing chair, in front of the desk.*

WILL. I'm terribly sorry. But you do see –

DAKER. *(suddenly)*: Sir William, what a charming boy that son of yours is.

A pause. There is a growing atmosphere of unease.

Is he at public school?

WILL. Yes.

DAKER. Ah... I'm afraid Joanie is hardly so fortunate.

WILL. *(horrified)*: She's at *school*?

DAKER. A council school, I'm ashamed to say, fate having dealt me some hard blows...*(fishing again in his pocket)* Here she is, in the school yard. Without, of course, the fox fur...*(he hands the snapshot to* WILL, *who stares at it)*

WILL. When was this taken?

DAKER. Three months ago. A week before the... party. *(after a pause)* Poor mite, when she was seven her mother left us, so she has missed the maternal guidance which I could hardly provide, could I trouble you for a little brandy? *(as* WILL *rises)* Even in these days, the battle of life is lost for a well bred girl who has been corrupted. It's broken me up...

He breaks down and sniffs: it is not genuine, but good enough to leave the other man abjectly uncomfortable.

WILL. I have said how deeply sorry I am. But I must insist –

DAKER. May I have my snapshot?

WILL looks down at it, then hands it back. DAKER puts it carefully away with the birth certificate, rises, and crosses to the drinks table.

WILL. I insist that if that girl stood in a court of law as she looked and talked that night –

DAKER. Sir William! *(waggishly)* That sinister expression!

WILL. What expression?

DAKER. 'Court of law'. *(helping himself to brandy)*

WILL. *(after a pause, sharply)* I don't quite know what you're after – but if it's money, you're wasting your time.

DAKER. *(looking at him, coldly)*: I don't follow you.

WILL. God knows I'm in no position to talk… but in a court of law, what you're trying on at the moment is covered by a fairly ugly word.

DAKER. My shabbiness has led you to misjudge me. Did you think I had come to extort money from you?

WILL. *(taken aback)*: It did sound like it –

DAKER. It's like this. After years of futile toil, I have learnt one lesson – that it is impossible to place a literary work without influence, preferably social. I understand, Sir William, that you have no pukka secretary?

WILL. *(after a pause, coldly, indicating the typing table)*: My man does pretty well –

DAKER. *(going to the typing table, and picking up a sheet of type-script)*: A half-educated jack-of-all-trades coping with a successful man of letters? 'Receive' spelt wrongly, some Sir William! Punctuation has always been my strong point, and – ergo – proof reading. I might even gradually take charge of Lady Trenting's correspondence? And might I not even run into your publisher here at dinner, he is another Cambridge man, I believe? I should be perfectly content with a shake down in your attic. *(as* **WILL** *sits again at the desk, gradually appalled)* I don't want to rush you. I votes you sleep on it, Sir William, and we meet tomorrow morning?

WILL. *(after a pause)*: Here.

DAKER. I would sooner – what about the bridge over the Serpentine?

WILL. *(sharply)*: Here. At twelve. If you're afraid I'll have Scotland Yard in that cupboard, you must take the risk.

DAKER. Scotland Ya – Sir William, what a wag you are – *(moving towards the main door)* – thank you so much –

WILL. Good-bye.

DAKER. *(stopping, taking his hat, and looking round)*: What a charming atmosphere. A room, I am sure, that grows on one.

Bowing, he goes out by the main door, shutting it softly behind him. **WILL** *looks after him, then rises; as if dazed, he crosses slowly towards the fireplace, his eyes alighting on the press-cutting book, as he passes it. A knock at the main door;* **ALBERT** *enters.*

ALBERT. Mrs. Tillyard, sir. Shall I ask her to join the others –

MARIAN *follows* **ALBERT** *from the hall; she is in a particularly smart new dress; hat and gloves.*

MARIAN. Hello, love – *(staring at his suit)* – but my darling Tramp, you look positively distinguished!

WILL *smiles mechanically, and stands at the fireplace; he seems still unable to take in what has happened.* **RONA** *comes downstairs and in at the main doorway;* **ALBERT** *waits for her to enter, then shuts the main door behind her, crosses and goes into the kitchen.* **RONA** *is now ready for going out, and carries hat and gloves.*

RONA. *(to* **MARIAN**): You're nice and early, good – *(giving* **WILL** *a quick look)*

MARIAN. They sent me the seating plan from The Savoy – my dear, I'm terrified, shan't eat a thing … Who was that on your doorstep, just going?

RONA. Who do you mean?

MARIAN. The strangest drip of a man. Said he hoped to meet again 'under your roof!

THE PARLOUR-MAID *enters from the kitchen, with a tray holding cocktail shaker, ice bucket and glasses, and takes it to the drinks table.*

RONA. *(to* MARIAN*)* Mix one of your specials, will you, darling?

MARIAN. I guessed a begging letter in person, the old touch –

WILL. Right first time.

MARIAN. They must be hell. How much did he want?

WILL. Ten thousand pounds.

MARIAN *laughs. The* MAID *goes back by the kitchen door.* RONA *looks at* WILL, *puzzled, as* MARIAN *mixes a cocktail.*

MARIAN. You forked out, of course!

WILL. I said 'Give me till tomorrow'.

MARIAN *laughs again. The main door opens, and* HAROLD *appears,* PHYLLIS *behind him.*

HAROLD. We thought we'd buzz off –

WILL. *(calling)*: Harold, Phyl – come in! *(as* HAROLD *comes in, followed by* PHYLLIS*)* Mrs Tillyard, Mr. and Mrs. Begham, great friends of mine all three. *(there is a bite in his voice)*

MARIAN. How do you do – you're just in time for a drink –

PHYLLIS. Goody goody – *(sitting on the sofa)*

RONA. *(to* HAROLD *and* PHYLLIS*)* Did you have enough to eat?

PHYLLIS. Oh, had a lovely tuck-in –

IAN *comes in from the hall, carrying a dog's lead.*

IAN. I'm going to take Bumper round the Square, is that all right?

RONA. You've only got five minutes darling –

IAN. And Dad, in case I forget when we get to Buckingham Palace, I thought I'd wish you good luck for this morning.

WILL. *(mechanically)*: Thank you, Ian.

> **PHYLLIS** *motions* **IAN** *to sit between her and* **HAROLD**, *on the sofa.*

IAN. *(to* **WILL***)*: Will you remember to ask him?

WILL. Ask him what?

IAN. If he's got that stamp.

RONA. He might not know, his father made the collection, you see –

MARIAN. And what's more, my lad, you can't ask Royalty a direct question.

IAN. Oh. *(to* **WILL***)* Could you work the conversation round?

WILL. *(turning to him, forcing a smile)*: I could try.

IAN. If you did ask a direct question, Dad, would you get into hot water?

> *The others laugh;* **WILL** *is looking at* **IAN**, *where he sits between* **PHYLLIS** *and* **HAROLD**, *and continues to look at him, fixedly.* **RONA** *sees the look.*

MARIAN. Jail, at the least. We'd go and smuggle your father bottles of rum — *(she also sees* **WILL***'s look, and stops)* What's the matter, Will?

IAN. Do we look funny?

WILL. *(after a pause, abruptly)*: Take Bumper for a walk, will you?

IAN. All right. *(rising)*: Shan't be long.

> *He runs out by the main door.*

RONA. *(to* **MARIAN***)*: Hurry with those drinks, dear.

MARIAN. Coming up! *(handing glasses)*

HAROLD. Let's get Bill plastered so he has to be poured out o' the car into the Palace, eh?

MARIAN. Lovely –

PHYLLIS. Don't – think o' the papers tonight!

MARIAN. *(drinking)*: Headlines right across the front page – let's think of a funny one –

WILL. 'Sir William Trenting Disgraced'.

A pause. **RONA** *is watching him, anxiously.*

MARIAN. *(disappointed)*: That sounds horrid without being funny.

RONA. I think so too – now if we adjourn to the drawing-room, I want Will to have a look at his speech, he's rather fussed about it.

MARIAN. Yes, of course –

HAROLD. *(going out by the main door, to* **MARIAN***)*: I've got a good one – 'A Dirty Knight at the Palace'.

PHYLLIS. *(following him)*: Oh Harold – *(giggling)* – isn't he awful…

MARIAN. *(laughing and turning to* **RONA***)*: But they're such fun, darling, who are they?

She follows them, out of the main door, and to the left. **RONA** *closes it behind her, puts down her hat and bag, and faces* **WILL**.

RONA. What was he after?

WILL. He wants to come and live with us.

RONA. No, seriously –

WILL. I am serious. He's a writer. He wants a job as my secretary.

RONA. *(after a pause)*: On what grounds?

WILL *starts to speak, then puts his glass down on the mantelpiece, goes to the main door and opens it.*

WILL. *(calling)*: Harold, you come in here a minute, will you?

HAROLD'S VOICE. *(in the drawing room)*: O.K, Bill –

HAROLD *comes back in by the main door, from the hall, carrying his glass.*

WILL. Harold, about the party.

HAROLD. The lunch? Oh, you couldn't ask *us* –

WILL. The Blue Lion party.

HAROLD. *(embarrassed, looking at* **RONA***)*: Oh…

WILL. *(after closing the main door, and coming back down to* **HAROLD***)*: D'you remember a girl there by the name of Joan? With her hair up on top – fox fur?

HAROLD. The one in the corner wi' you? *(to* **RONA** *abashed)* Sorry…

RONA. Harold, say everything that has to be said – *please…*

WILL. *(to* **HAROLD***)*: Have you any idea who brought her?

HAROLD. Me an' my pal Ed.

WILL. *You* did? Well, how old would *you* think she was?

HAROLD. Hard to say. You see, I knew?

WILL. *(after a pause, incredulously)*: You knew?

HAROLD. She goes to school round the corner, wi' my young brother.

RONA. School?

WILL. *(to her)*: She's fourteen. *(to* **HAROLD**, *as* **RONA** *turns away.)* But if you knew her age, why didn't you tell me?

HAROLD. Sorry, Bill, I though you knew, same as everybody else –

WILL. Everybody else?

HAROLD. Ed and me'd been havin' a bet with 'em all in the bar, as to whether we'd get her up to your room.

WILL. You saw her walk over to me – you saw what went on – and you thought I *knew?*

HAROLD. Sorry, Bill… *(lamely)* I remember Ed sayin' to me, "Old Bill's a one", he said, "wi' one as young as that, but she's for the high jump sometime", an' then he said, "Good mind to make a date there myself!"

WILL. Did he?

HAROLD. For the next night… Fixin' the camera, we was. *(shamefaced, as* **WILL** *stares at him, and* **RONA** *looks bewildered from one to the other)* Well, after all…

WILL. After all what?

HAROLD. With you so free-an'-easy, Bill, an' eggin' us all on, we got the idea that you…

His voice trails away. A pause. WILL *moves slowly towards the desk.*

WILL. I don't think I can be as free-and-easy as I thought. *(looking out of the window)* O.K. Harold, my fault…

HAROLD *looks at* RONA, *and goes out by the main door, closing it behind him.* WILL *and* RONA *look at each other.*

This man's her father. He's coming again tomorrow morning.

RONA. Blackmail. You've read about it, and when it happens…

WILL. *(looking at the desk)*: We just had a sensible talk. *(walking towards her)* It felt more and more horrible in this room…but that's all it was. *(looking at her)* And here we are, having a sensible talk. But I'm looking at a tiny muscle in your forehead, that I noticed that time Ian had the appendix. It's throbbing now.

RONA. Ian got better. *(as* WILL *moves abruptly, and looks again out of the window)* If we keep our heads, we're all right –

WILL. You said I was on thin ice, remember?

RONA. *(distressed)*: I was angry –

WILL. *(turning and looking at her, slow and dazed)*: Is the ice… cracking?

RONA. Don't blame yourself for what's happened this morning –

WILL. I don't mean just that – has it all caught up with me? *(bewildered)* But I haven't meant any harm… have I?

RONA. I know you haven't, my darling…

WILL. And I *have* a conscience, about money, and loyalty and all that – you've often told me I had too many scruples… But I've never felt that any of *this* was really wrong, so long as you knew…

RONA. You see, Will, one ends by harming without meaning to.

WILL. *(after a pause)*: Overnight, I've turned a child of fourteen… into a whore.

RONA. Will…

WILL. I thought just now… why shouldn't that boy of ours –

RONA. *(upset)*: Don't, Will, don't bring Ian into it… The side of you that belongs to him and to me has nothing to do with what we're up against now –

WILL. But in the end it *must* have… Just now, looking at him, I remembered how many times, after a drink, I've felt great easy tears come into my eyes, as I thought 'That funny sensitive creature is my son' – sensitive, mark you, I realised that! But have I once faced the fact that I'm his father? I'm having to face it now… Why shouldn't he have been born the child of this man today? He'd have had a grim beginning, but he'd have weathered it. He hears one night that round at the pub there's a mad party, given by a rich cheery – *(breaking down)* – I can't go this morning, I can't…

IAN *comes in by the main door, from the hall, followed by* MARIAN, *from the left.* WILL *controls himself, with a desperate effort, and walks to the fireplace.*

IAN. I took Bumper, and there's a man at the door.

MARIAN. *(putting on her fur)*: Thank you, dear, that'll be my hired car, I'm calling on a few friends to boast about the luncheon –

ALBERT *appears at the kitchen door, in his chauffeur's uniform, his cap under his arm, carrying a top-hat and a clothes brush.*

ALBERT. All right, sir?

IAN. It isn't a hired car, it's a reporter.

RONA *turns and looks at him; he sits in the arm-chair and pulls up his socks.*

RONA. A reporter?

She looks to **ALBERT***, who hands the top-hat to her and goes out by the main doorway, into the hall.*

MARIAN. Reporters – *(to* **IAN***)* – my dear, what it is to visit the houses of the great. *(to* **RONA***)* Shall I talk to them, darling, and tell them Will's pressed for time?

RONA. *(looking at* **WILL***)* But they did all that on New Year's Day …

ALBERT *returns.*

ALBERT. It's a photographer, my lady – if you and Sir William would mind posing on the doorstep before you leave for the Palace.

A pause.

MARIAN. *(going)*: Lovely, we'll snoop through the dining-room curtains – come on, Ian, have a look at the aristocracy!

IAN. *(making to follow her)*: Rather fun –

RONA. Ian!

IAN. *(stopping)*: Yes, Mummy?

RONA. *(smoothing his hair)*: Straighten your tie –

IAN. But you don't like me being in pictures in the paper –

RONA. This is special. Your father isn't sent for by the King every day.

She goes to **WILL***, gives him the top hat, takes up her hat and bag, takes* **IAN***'s arm, and goes out with him and* **MARIAN** *into the hall.*

(going) I feel quite sentimental about today, isn't it silly –

IAN. *(going)*: I wonder if it'll be in any of the papers we take –

MARIAN. *(going)*: Mind you keep a straight face, Master Ian –

Their voices die away. **WILL** *looks round the room, quickly, desperately. He looks down at the top hat in his hand, makes a great effort, puts it on and follows.*

The curtain falls, and rises immediately on…

Scene Five

The next morning: noon.

Bright winter sunlight. The main door is open. From the drawing-room beyond, on the left, faint gramophone music: a dance tune. **HAROLD** *sits in the arm-chair smoking, and idly reading one of the uniform editions of* **WILL**'s *novels.* **ALBERT** *comes downstairs and into the room, carrying* **WILL**'s *morning suit, on the hanger.*

ALBERT. What you readin', chum?

HAROLD. *(looking at the spine of the book)*: The Works of Will Trenting, Vol. Seven.

ALBERT. *(looking over at the book)*: The Deep Meadow. Mm.

HAROLD. Too deep for me. Except the 'ot stuff.

ALBERT. 'Ot stuff's universal… *(going to the cupboard and hanging up the hanger)* Where's Phyllis?

HAROLD. In the lounge, playin' the gramophone. She asked if she could.

ALBERT. *(picking up a batch of newspaper cuttings from the typing table)*: D'you know why you're here this morning?

HAROLD. 'Cause we got a wire, fat'ead, askin' us up.

ALBERT. I know that, Sex-box; I sent it – *(closing the main door, as the music dies away)* I mean what they want you up for.

HAROLD. Bill told us just now – to face up to this chap when he comes.

ALBERT. It's a nice how-d'you-do, Harold, isn't it?

HAROLD. It sure is. How is he?

ALBERT. Stayed in last night, an' never had a drink. I don't fancy that.

HAROLD. How long have you seen this comin', Albert?

ALBERT. Fifteen years. There was nothing I could do, except press his trousers an' hope for the best. The chances he's took! Take the way I got this job. Met him in a pub.

HAROLD. No!

ALBERT. Up comes the guv, a bit round the bend, and says "You've got an intelligent eye, old chap, see me tomorrow morning, what are we all drinkin'?" An intelligent eye, always remembered that.

HAROLD. Did he say anything about the other one? *(laughing heartily)*

ALBERT. He meant both, it's literary... But the risk! If I'd been a wide boy –

HAROLD. Turn it up, you was a wide boy!

ALBERT. All right, I was a wide boy... but I've gone straight since – but how was he to know I'd go straight, just because I got a honest face?

HAROLD. You hit the nail, Albert. I got a honest face too, an' look at me!

ALBERT. That's right. How far would a wide boy get without a honest face? *(he crosses to the fireplace, and props the cuttings up on the mantelpiece)*

HAROLD. You know, Albert, it's funny about these upper classes. No end o' sophisticated devils, right? Well, when it comes to a spot o' trouble, they're a bunch of worried kids. You and me'd be takin' this at a gentle trot. Why is that?

ALBERT. *(at the fireplace)* Because we're something born an' not made. Men o' the world. I mean, take tarts –

The main door opens, and **RONA** *enters; she looks tired.*

HAROLD *rises.*

RONA. Get me an aspirin, Albert, will you?

ALBERT. *(the perfect servant)* Yes, my lady.

He goes out by the kitchen door. **HAROLD** *puts his book back in its place on the desk, as* **RONA** *crosses to the windows, opens one, and calls.*

RONA. It's gone twelve... Good morning, Harold, it was nice of you to come up.

HAROLD. Not at all, least we could do. I'll tell Phyl you're down.

He wanders out by the main door and to the left. **RONA** *crosses restlessly, and sits on the sofa.* **THANE** *comes in by the windows.*

THANE. Will and I must have been round the garden fifty times.

WILL *follows him; he too looks tired, but is dressed carefully and seems to have groomed himself for an ordeal. He closes the window.*

RONA. Have you been talking?

THANE. I have.

WILL. Tactics. I've been thinking. Sizing up... what I've been doing.

THANE. *(looking from one to the other)*: I'll get the others in.

He goes out by the main door and shuts it behind him. **RONA** *and* **WILL** *look at each other.*

WILL. *(the words gradually coming out, nervous, careful)*: I've prided myself on my honesty, haven't I, all along... I made myself believe that if I could write about these things and get away with it, I could live with them too. *(looking round the room.)*: And on top of that I kidded myself I was entitled to live with this, as well. This knighthood, how *could* I have said 'yes' to it?

RONA. You did it to please me –

WILL. But it was cheating. After sixteen years of cheating... the climax. Cast your mind back to when we first met. I liked living in the mud, and I didn't care who knew it. Trenting the Tramp. But I was a physical wreck, it was killing my work. So I got married. And that gave me security, steadied me down. Damned useful. I had it both ways.

RONA. Don't...

WILL. *(crossing to the fireplace, and looking at the photograph)*: A wife, a son, a home – how *could* I have thought I had a right to them, as well as to the other? If I liked the mud so much, the least I could have done was stay in it. *(looking round)* I don't belong here.

RONA. *(rising, and going to him)*: Don't say that, you'll break my heart…

THANE enters by the main door, followed by HAROLD *and* PHYLLIS. RONA *controls herself.* WILL *picks up the newspaper cuttings from the mantelpiece.*

WILL. Come in, Thane – sit down, you two… *(reading)* 'Sir William's luncheon speech lacked the usual shock tactics; Will Trenting was – dare we breathe it – sedate.'

PHYLLIS has sat on the sofa; HAROLD *sits on the right arm of it, next to her.* WILL *and* RONA *are standing at the fireplace.*

RONA. Oh dear, isn't that nice… Darling, I *was* proud of you –

THANE. Shall we dispense with the press cuttings, and get down to the blackmail? … The legal position is clear; the evidence is strong enough to establish the wilful procuring of a person under the age of consent.

RONA. It wasn't wilful –

THANE. I am anticipating the attitude of a British jury.

RONA. I'm sorry –

ALBERT enters from the kitchen, with aspirins and a glass of water, which he gives to RONA.

THANE. I suggest bluff to start with, good and hard – *(to RONA)* – does Albert know?

RONA. Stay, will you, Albert, when he comes?

ALBERT. Yes, my lady.

THANE. The more of us the better –

ALBERT. I'll just watch the front door.

RONA. Good, better if you let him in…

ALBERT goes out by the main door, closing it behind him.

WILL. *(cheering up)* I've only to imply that Rona has always known everything, and so have a few other people, and what have I to lose – and he'll go down like a balloon –

THANE. That's the line. Let's bear in mind that most blackmailers are (a) unintelligent and (b) easily scared. Watch his face when you introduce me as a barrister. He's not to know I gave it up years ago –

ALBERT appears at the main door.

ALBERT. The gentleman's here, my lady.

THANE. Ask him in, will you, Albert?

ALBERT goes out into the hall, to the right.

RONA. *(to WILL)* Have a drink, darling.

WILL. I want to keep a clear head. Better late than never.

ALBERT. *(in the main doorway)* Mr. Daker.

DAKER passes him, entering from the hall. He looks much as he did the previous day.

DAKER. Good morning – *(seeing that WILL is by no means alone)* – oh…

WILL. Mr. Daker, you've met my wife.

RONA sits on the sofa, next to PHYLLIS. ALBERT closes the main door and takes his stand in the room; he does this unobtrusively, but the click of the door does not escape DAKER's notice.

May I present Mrs. Begham, Mr. Begham, Mr. Lampeter, and behind you Mr. Ross, all *au fait* with our little problem?

DAKER. How do you do – *(in a flurry of timidity – is there a glass of steel behind it? – it is hard to say)* – I was hardly prepared for this pleasure, I feel quite nervous –

WILL. *(pouring a brandy)* Mr Daker, I think I know your tipple?

DAKER. *(sitting in the arm-chair)* That's most thoughtful of you… Lady Trenting, how delightfully Sir William's speech came over yesterday! In spite of the fact that the radio in the Blue Lion is hardly – *(taking the brandy from HAROLD, who has been handed it by WILL)* – salutations, everybody!

He drinks.

THANE. *(who is leaning against the desk)* Have you seen Mr. Begham before?

DAKER. Begham – *(looking uncertainly at* **ALBERT***)*

HAROLD. Blue Lion.

DAKER. *(to him)* We should wear an old pub tie, don't you know…

THANE. Harold knows your daughter too. His friend Ed spent the night with her, twenty-four hours after the Blue Lion party.

DAKER. Indeed.

THANE. I suggest that was quick work for a girl who wasn't already inclined to vice?

DAKER. *(in apparent distress)* That's a painful thing to say to a father, don't you agree, Sir William? I don't understand how you can – *(to* **HAROLD***, referring to* **THANE***)* – who is that gentleman?

THANE. I'm a barrister.

A pause. **DAKER** *looks at* **THANE***; the others watch.*

DAKER. What a coincidence, I am a barrister, too. *(Drinking)*

WILL. You?

DAKER. Retired, worse luck. *(to* **THANE***)* As you are also, sir, no doubt- you have the retired look, if I may say so… *(giving his empty glass back to* **HAROLD***, and fumbling in his pocket.)* To return to my little girl… I wonder if any of you have any news of her?

RONA. How do you mean?

DAKER. I arrived home yesterday to find this note. *(bringing out a piece of paper)* Rather upsetting. *(reading)* 'Dear Pop, I've buzzed off with Ed that dated me up at Bill's party, I'm O.K, Joan'. Her style is tainted with the cinema.

WILL *turns abruptly and takes a drink.*

THANE. She mentions – that evening?

DAKER. *(showing the paper, and spelling)* 'B-I-L-L' Alias Will… Ed is a stoker, a married man. Rather upsetting.

He puts the paper away again, carefully.

She was doing well at school, Lady Trenting, and this –

WILL. *(turning and loosing his temper)* For God's sake drop this title business and talk straight!

THANE. *(quietening him)* Will… *(to **DAKER**)* Cards on the table, Mr. Daker. How much will you settle for?

DAKER. Settle?

THANE. Pounds, shillings and pence. Five hundred pounds.

DAKER. *(after a pause, to **WILL**)* Sir William – *(as **WILL** makes a gesture)* – I'm sorry if your title offends you, but I know of no other way to address you… I fail to see what I did yesterday to prompt this. You pressed money on me, which I refused – then out of the blue you suggested a job. Should I have refused that too?

THANE. *(to the others, shaking his head)* It's because you're all witnesses –

WILL. He hasn't studied law for nothing.

***THANE** moves away from **DAKER**, frustrated.*

DAKER. I'm sorry, but –

*He stops, as **HAROLD** rises slowly and faces him; **HAROLD** is holding **DAKER**'s empty glass at an angle which makes it look dangerously like a weapon. **DAKER** rises.*

What's the game?

His tone is different; he and the younger man might be standing in a saloon bar, on the edge of an ugly scene.

HAROLD. *(to **DAKER**)* Ever heard o' blokes bein' beaten up?

DAKER. *(retreating to the foot of the desk)* Who d'you think –

HAROLD. *(following him)* Bigger people than you been found wi' their throats cut.

DAKER. Are you threatening me?

***RONA** covers her ears, involuntarily.*

HAROLD. Just a warnin', pal. You don't have to spend ninepence in the flicks to see the gangsters.

*The main door opens, and **IAN** enters.*

IAN. Excuse me, I left my fountain pen.

He goes to the sofa, fishes a pen from a hiding-place deep in the side of it, and goes out again, closing the main door behind him.

A pause; **WILL** *crosses to* **HAROLD**.

WILL. Thank you, Harold, but it's no good.

DAKER. *(to* **WILL***)* May I see you alone?

WILL *looks quickly from* **RONA** *to* **THANE**. **RONA** *rises.*

RONA. We'll go in the other room –

RONA *hurries out by the main door, and to the left, followed by* **PHYLLIS**, **THANE** *follows them, and waits in the main doorway.*

HAROLD. *(to* **WILL***)* Blokes do get bumped off in this country. There was one three weeks back, hundred yards from the Blue Lion. *(to* **DAKER**.*)* Remember?

WILL. Sorry, Harold.

HAROLD *looks regretful, and goes out by the main door, to the left.* **THANE** *follows him.*

ALBERT. *(again the perfect servant)* Would there be anything else sir?

WILL. No thank you, Albert.

ALBERT *follows the others, closing the main door.* **WILL** *faces* **DAKER**, *who crosses and helps himself to brandy.*

DAKER. I'm so grateful, I have a phobia about crowds –

WILL. *(sitting at the desk)* It'll save time if you stop being a humbug for two minutes. You're on the wrong beam – I'm not a little country curate who's been caught in the act. I'm a tough customer with a wife who's got no illusions, and some tough friends.

DAKER. Is your son tough too? *(he sits in* **ALBERT***'s typing chair in front of the desk; a pause)* You have put ideas into my head, Sir William. An offer of five hundred pounds has temptations.

WILL. *(looking at him)* Oh.

He rises and crosses to **RONA***'s desk, taking out his fountain pen.*

Would you mind dropping me a line setting forth roughly how you intend to spend it?

DAKER. I have a phobia about letters too, isn't it ridiculous?

WILL. Oh. *(unlocking a drawer in the desk and taking out a cheque book)*

DAKER. I tell you what – if you'd be kind enough to drop me a line, offering to lend me the money – eh?

WILL. Your phobia only applies to the writing end? I see…

DAKER. I can't feel at ease with that little movement of the wrist – *(chuckling)* – ha ha…

WILL. *(writing)* Your first name?

DAKER. William.

WILL. *(writing)* We have one thing in common.

DAKER. Oh – if you'd be good enough to write your *letter* first.

WILL. I get your point…

He takes a sheet of writing paper from a rack on **RONA***'s desk, and writes; his back is to* **DAKER**. **DAKER** *looks slowly round the room, then takes another drink. His eyes go to* **WILL***'s desk. He crosses to the desk, and sits at it. He sees before him the uniform edition, places his arms slowly around the books, and looks around the room. He is in the master's place at last.*

WILL *looks doubtfully at the last few words he has written, rises, and walks across towards his desk, holding his pen and studying his letter.*
(reading) 'Dear Daker, I hear your financial position' et cetera et cetera…' I have always made a point of helping' – no, too pompous…*(Thinking)* 'I have been lucky myself' – that's better – 'and you have not'…

He looks for something to rest the letter on, takes out one of the books in the uniform edition, and sits (to write) on **ALBERT***'s typing chair, formerly occupied by* **DAKER**.

DAKER. *(as* WILL *writes)* When you turned then, did you observe that I am sitting at your desk? *(he is drunk, but his manner is suddenly simple and direct)*

WILL. *(looking at him)* I suppose I did, subconsciously. *(writing)* Why?

DAKER. I wanted to see if it gave me a feeling of power. *(as* WILL *looks at him)* Of owning this room. *(looking at the uniform edition)* Owning you. While your back was to me, I had that feeling. Like being drunk, only better. Then you turned round again. You're sitting where I sat. Writing to my dictation. But I haven't got a feeling of power.

WILL. Because a blackmailer is beneath contempt. *(going back to his letter.)* What an odd little man you are.

He goes on writing. He has said it with a tolerant disdain, almost kindly, which seals his fate.

Writing with sarcasm.

'You must not, as a self-respecting member of society, be offended by a cheque...

DAKER. *(suddenly)* I've changed my mind, I don't want the money.

WILL *looks at him incredulously, then down at the letter.*

WILL. How do I know you won't change your mind back?

DAKER. You heard what I said. I don't want the money.

WILL. What can I say, except 'Have a brandy?' *(he rises, lays down the letter and pen, and puts back the book.)*

DAKER. No, I want to be clear enough to get me through what I've got to say.

WILL. But what can there be left to say?

DAKER. You don't seem to understand. I am going on with the case.

WILL. You're what?

DAKER. I am going to give you a charge.

WILL. You can't mean it.

DAKER. And I shall not change my mind. *(as* **WILL** *sits, slowly)* Because I can feel it creeping back. The power. Warming me, lifting me… Yesterday morning, you asked me about my writing, d'you remember? But what you don't recall is the patronage in those four words 'Have you written much?' Did you sleep last night? *I* didn't. I got up and started drinking. I pulled a trunk from under the bed and heaved it over. There was a smell of musty paper that knocked you down. I started to calculate. Two million and a half dead words. This lot – *(showing the bound volumes)* – and half as many again. Stuffed down the side, the letters saying no-no-no. I found yours.

WILL. Mine?

DAKER. Twelve years ago. 'It's kinder to be frank, your work is worthy but dull, you are not a writer.'

WILL. An opinion I seem to have shared with quite a few –

DAKER. *(rising, in a towering rage)* How dared you write that to me? It was calling a spade a spade, wasn't it – down with bloody middle-class scruples, up sincerity! Then you had success, didn't you? Wife, son, house in Regent's Park, Nobel Prize, respect – all the things the failures are allowed to gape at… but watch us try and get near – keep off the grass! But have you responsibilities?

WILL. Don't… don't say it…

DAKER. No, you're the exception – down to the jolly old pub, get a bunch of the girls and boys, this round's on me, turn the lights out, no bloody middle-class scruples… And then back to the loving wife, and Sir William this and Sir William that – while the flotsam and jetsam stand in the rain, watching you waltz from swings to roundabouts and back – and you *dare* to call *me* a humbug! *(mimicking viciously)* 'Your work is worthy but dull, what an odd little man you are'… No, I shall not change my mind.

He fumbles in a pocket and extracts a grimy piece of paper. RONA *hurries in by the main door, shutting it behind her.*

RONA. You've been shouting –

DAKER. *(his manner again nervous and polite)* Lady Trenting, please come in – may I use your telephone, rather urgent – *(taking up the telephone and dialling the number on the paper)*

RONA. What happened?

WILL. *(after an agonised look at her, to* DAKER*)* I'm not begging for your mercy for myself; but for my son. My wife's son. He has never harmed a living soul.

DAKER. *(staring at him coldly)* The harm has been done already. To my daughter.

WILL. *(after a pause, in a wild outburst of pleading)* Please!

DAKER *is standing at the telephone, looking down at the uniform edition on the desk. He touches one of the books.*

DAKER. A present from you, Lady Trenting? What exquisite bindings… *(into the telephone)* Is that Whitehall 7459?… *(sitting slowly, into the desk chair.)* You won't know who I am, but I want to secure an appointment with the Director of Public Prosecutions…

The curtain falls, and rises immediately on…

Scene Six

Three days later; late afternoon, the light is going.
ALBERT *is waiting at the telephone, holding an address*
book. **RONA** *sits on the sofa, deep in thought; she holds*
an open letter in one hand, and has not moved for
some time. **IAN** *sits at* **RONA***'s desk; he is addressing an*
envelope. He takes up a book from the stool, and slides it
into the envelope.

ALBERT. *(into the telephone)* All right, I'll hang on…

RONA. Isn't that one of Daddy's?

IAN. Henderson asked me to send him one, so I bought it with my book token.

RONA. Henderson?

IAN. You remember, he shares my study at school. He's heard Dad's books aren't bad.

RONA. Oh…*(looking at her letter)*

IAN. *(seeing it)* But that's the school notepaper!

RONA. It's from Mr. Gates, he's getting those three seats for the school play next term.

IAN. *(pleased)* Oh good! I must put a note in for Henderson… *(as* **RONA** *puts the letter aside, thoughtfully)* Mummy, you don't seem very interested.

RONA. *(quickly)* Yes I am darling, I'm delighted…*(as* **IAN** *starts to scribble a note.)* Are you looking forward to next term?

IAN. Rather!

ALBERT. *(into the telephone, in his butler's voice)* If you could say Lady Trenting's in bed wi' the 'flu and can't dine, she's very sorry.

IAN. *(looking up at* **RONA***)* Was that a white lie?

RONA. Yes.

IAN. Don't they always get found out?

RONA. Not if your conscience is clear.

ALBERT. *(into the telephone)* In Harrods? Can't have been Lady Trenting, they say we all got a double, don't they, she's in bed wi' the flu an' very very sorry.

He hangs up, with a cluck of impatience, and puts the address book away in **RONA***'s bag.*

I phoned the lot now, my lady –

RONA. Thank you, Albert.

IAN. *Why* don't you want to go out, Mummy?

RONA. I'm tired, dear, that's all –

A rat-tat at the front door. She and **ALBERT** *look at each other;* **IAN** *finishes his letter, slips it into the envelope with the book, and seals the envelope.*

ALBERT. It'll be the evening paper.

RONA. Get it, will you?

ALBERT *goes out by the main door, to the right, leaving it open. (to* **IAN***, going to the wardrobe, with an effort at briskness)*

Ian, would you like to take your father's overcoat?

IAN. Why doesn't he come in? I've never seen him sit in the garden before –

RONA. He's thinking out a plot.

She looks anxiously towards the main doorway.

IAN. Would he tell me, so I can tell it in the dormitory next term?

RONA. *(taking* **WILL***'s overcoat from the wardrobe)* He might. Why don't you ask him?

IAN. Good idea –

RONA. *(taking a rug)* And wrap this round yourself –

IAN *takes the overcoat and the rug, opens the window and hurries out.* **RONA** *shuts the window behind him.* **ALBERT** *comes back, turning pages of the* Evening News, *and scanning them.*

Well?

ALBERT. I can't find anything, my lady.

RONA. Thank God. So we're all right till the morning. You're sure there were no photographers?

ALBERT. Outside the – the police court? Quite sure, my lady. *(taking a small bouquet from under his arm)* And there was a messenger with this.

RONA. *(taking the flowers)* Aren't they nice, it means nobody's heard yet, anyway – *(reading the card)* – but Albert, they're from you!

ALBERT. *(stiffly)* Yes, my lady.

Near tears, she kisses him.

I think that was the front door, my lady. *(opening the main door)*

RONA. It'll be Mrs. Tillyard. I must freshen up.

She hurries out of the main door and upstairs, taking the flowers with her. **ALBERT** *moves and looks out of the window. A pause; the* **MAID** *enters by the main door, and* **MARIAN** *follows her. She looks shocked and worried. The* **MAID** *takes her coat.*

MARIAN. Thank you…

The **MAID** *closes the door from the outside.*

Good evening, Albert.

ALBERT. Good evening, madam.

MARIAN. Lady Trenting is in, is she?

ALBERT. She's expecting you, madam, she won't be a moment.

A pause. **MARIAN** *sits on the sofa.*
(holding it out) The evening paper, madam?

MARIAN. *(looking from him to the paper)* Oh… Thank you, Albert.

She takes the paper. **ALBERT** *goes into the kitchen.* **MARIAN** *looks at the paper anxiously, then takes another copy of the same paper (folded) out of her bag, and compares the two.*

THE PARLOUR MAID *opens the main door.* THANE *passes her and comes into the room; the* MAID *closes the door from the outside.* THANE *is in time to see* MARIAN *make to put her copy hurriedly back into her bag.*

THANE. You've seen it?

MARIAN. Yes. Theirs is the early edition. *(taking out her copy again)* 'Out on Bail'… It must be a hideous mistake.

THANE. *(carefully as she reads)* Though Will's often managed to shock suburbia, hasn't he? And haven't we – as his friends – encouraged him to, a bit?

MARIAN. You mean debunking the authorities, that sort of thing? Of course we have, it was part of his act as a writer – but what has that got to do with – *(holding out the paper in amazement)* – East End orgies – newly created knight and schoolgirl – obscene photographs… My dear Thane – *(bewildered)* – it's a frame up!

THANE. I'm sorry for Rona.

MARIAN. But what a blessing she's a sophisticated woman who'll believe *him* and not *this*!

RONA *comes in at the main door; she is fastening a necklace.*

RONA. *(to* MARIAN*)* Darling, I'll get you a drink – *(seeing* THANE, *surprised)* – Thane!

THANE. You don't mind?

RONA. Don't be silly, but it's not going to be fun. I want Marian to know before everybody else does –

The telephone rings. RONA *goes towards it.*

MARIAN. *(quickly)* Don't answer, Rona.

RONA. Why not?

THANE. It's in the later edition.

MARIAN *holds out her newspaper.* RONA *looks from her to the telephone, braces herself, goes to the kitchen door, opens it, and calls.*

RONA. Albert!

ALBERT hurries in from the kitchen, passes her and goes to the telephone.

ALBERT. *(into the telephone)* Sir William Trenting's house, yes… *(startled, to* **RONA**, *his hand over the mouthpiece)* The press. *(as* **RONA** *shakes her head at him, into the telephone)* Very sorry, out of town for the night.

He hangs up, and looks at Rona.

RONA. *(to* **ALBERT***)* It's in the later edition.

ALBERT. Oh.

RONA. Switch off the bell, will you, and say the same to everybody.

ALBERT. Yes, my lady.

He switches off the telephone bell, and goes out by the kitchen door, closing it behind him.

THANE. Did I hear somebody in the drawing-room?

RONA. Phyllis and Harold. They're playing cards in there – she was so upset on the phone this morning, I asked them up. *(turning to* **MARIAN***)*

MARIAN. Darling, we're all with you. If it gives you any comfort, I'm speaking for everybody who knows you both, and loves you.

RONA. *(moved)* I wanted to hear that.

MARIAN. But who *invented* it?

RONA. How do you mean, invented?

MARIAN. The whole implication – *(holding out the paper)* – 'may develop into a Jekyll and Hyde case' – you've never read anything so fantastic!

RONA. *(after a pause)* It would be mean not to tell you. Anyway there'll be the evidence. It's… not invented.

MARIAN. Not… But there's a picture of this child, in her school clothes – Rona, she's *fourteen!*

RONA. *(wearily)* It never occurred to him she wasn't ten years older, but it'll be hard to prove… And he didn't take the pictures. Apart from that, it's true.

MARIAN. My god…

THANE. Where is he?

> RONA *looks out of the window. It has begun to grow dark.*

RONA. In the garden. I wish he'd have a drink. He's sitting talking to Ian.

MARIAN. He's not – telling him – ?

RONA. Not yet *(as* THANE *joins her)* Ian looks too happy for that, don't you think? He's making up a plot for him. *(turning, and seeing* MARIAN*'s face)* Mr. Hyde – and Doctor Jekyll. *(looking back)*

THANE. How absorbed they both look.

RONA. And one not much older than the other. *(as they both watch)* Wouldn't it be nice, Thane, if I could keep them behind glass, forever?

MARIAN. *(incredulously)* Rona, are you asking me to believe that when Will used to go off for a weekend, and we all joked about the steady blonde he was hiding from you, it was – this?

RONA. Except that he's never hidden it from me.

MARIAN. You've – known?

RONA. It was always understood that Will should lead his own life side by side with his life with me… I'm making it sound awful, but we knew what we meant, and it worked. *(her voice breaking)* I thought it did…

MARIAN. He would only marry you on those terms? *(as* RONA *bites her lip)* Darling, I'm sounding awful now –

RONA. Would you sooner it was the steady blonde?

MARIAN. I'm sorry, Rona –

RONA. No Marian, I'm serious. I want some idea of the way our friends are going to take this. Suppose that for years, behind my back, in cold blood, my husband had been carrying on with another woman… suppose I suddenly found out that this poor creature was bringing up a child by him – it's been known! Would you think that more excusable? With a sporting chance of his making three people wretched for life – me, the woman, and her child… would you call *that* a better marriage?

A pause – **MARIAN** *rises.*

MARIAN. You mean me and Gerald?

RONA. Oh…*(realising she had hit too near the mark)* I wasn't actually – *(defiantly)* – if you like.

MARIAN. I'm sorry, but I've come to accept Gerald. He's my husband, and that's that. Nobody could accuse me of being strait-laced, over a weakness I can understand –

THANE. *(gently)* But, Marian, haven't we all, at some time or other, been startled by a weakness in *ourselves?* By a sudden stir in the blood that just catches you off your guard?

RONA. Of course we have! *(to* **MARIAN***)* *I* have, I know… And they're things we'd be appalled to see in the paper – but does it put us beyond the pale? *(still to* **MARIAN***)* Haven't you one thing like that – I don't even mean sex – *haven't* you? *(as* **MARIAN** *does not answer)* I'm sorry. I've gone too far.

The main door opens abruptly, and **HAROLD** *hurries in.*

HAROLD. We just heard Albert on the 'phone –

PHYLLIS runs past **HAROLD***, from the left.*

PHYLLIS. It's in the paper about us, isn't it awful?

MARIAN *looks down at her paper, quickly.*

RONA. *(to* **HAROLD** *and* **PHYLLIS***)* I'm sorry you had to be mentioned –

PHYLLIS. *(sitting next to* **MARIAN***)* Makes you feel terrible, doesn't it?

She sees **MARIAN** *staring from her to* **HAROLD** *and back, and is instinctively silent.* **MARIAN** *rises. An awkward pause.*

We oughtn't to be here.

HAROLD. *(to* **RONA***)* I told her not to ring up.

RONA. *(fiercely)* You have a right to be here, that's why I asked for you. We're in this together.

THANE. *(at the window)* They're getting up.

RONA. *(as* **MARIAN** *moves to the main door)* No, see him for a minute –

MARIAN. Don't you think it'd be more tactful…*(her voice trailing away)*

RONA. I was assuming there's no need for tact when old friends are in trouble.

MARIAN. My darling… *(almost in tears)* What can I say that doesn't sound stuffy and vile… But I'm terribly taken aback, I can't pretend I'm not –

The click of the window; **IAN** *enters carrying his rug.*

RONA. Was it a good plot, darling?

IAN. Wonderful. Shall I tell it?

RONA. Not now, Ian – and would you leave the rug on your bed?

IAN. *(looking at the wardrobe cupboard)* But doesn't it belong –

RONA. Yes, but I want it up there now.

IAN. Hello, Auntie Marian – I've got the seats for you and Mummy for the play next term, did she tell you?

MARIAN. *(with an effort)* Have you, dear? Good…

IAN goes out by the main door, **RONA** *closing it behind him. She turns on the lights,* **WILL** *enters from the garden, wearing his overcoat. He looks tired, almost listless. He closes that window behind him, and is in the middle of taking off his overcoat when he sees* **MARIAN**'s *face.*

RONA. Will, it's in the paper.

WILL *looks at her. She takes* **MARIAN**'s *paper, crosses to him and unfolds it.*

I haven't seen it either.

WILL takes her hand; she stands next to him at the desk, and spreads the paper on the desk so that they see the whole of the front page. WILL braces himself, and looks.

WILL. *(reading, then looking up)* Phyllis, Harold... I'm sorry. *(reading)* Is Albert coping with the phone?

RONA. Yes... Thane, would you watch in case Ian comes down?

THANE. Of course.

He goes out by the main door, closing it. WILL looks up, then looks at the uniform edition in front of him.

WILL. For years, off and on, I've been well-known as a writer. For the next two hours, I know – I don't even have to take a bet – I *know* that in London one human being out of three will be talking about *me*. That's *real* fame. My ears aren't burning, but my head's buzzing. Slight claustrophobia... It was nice of you to come, Marian.

MARIAN. I'm sorry, Will. *(coming forward)* Anything I can do ... *(she and WILL look at each other)*

WILL. I was supposed to be honest as the day, wasn't I? I've cheated. Marian, I didn't mean to...

He looks out of the window. MARIAN tries to speak, but cannot. She puts her arms round RONA, abruptly kisses her, and (almost in tears) hurries out by the main door, shutting the door behind her.

PHYLLIS. Poor thing... It's a blow for their friends, Harold, isn't it?

WILL. It's a blow for you too.

PHYLLIS. It's not quite the same with us... *(philosophically)* I do hope we don't get a whopper of a sentence.

HAROLD. *(equally philosophically)* Might be a fine, Thane said, or might be a month.

PHYLLIS. A month isn't *so* bad.

WILL. What'd you do with your little girl?

PHYLLIS. Brenda? She'll go to her gran, like she did… that other time.

HAROLD. Gran spoils her o' course, but then so does her mum.

WILL *and* RONA *look at each other, and laugh.*

RONA. *(thoughtfully)* We're laughing.

HAROLD. Takes your mind off, doesn't it?

ALBERT *comes in by the kitchen door: he looks as if he had just lost his temper.*

ALBERT. About dinner, my lady.

RONA. Oh. Cook knows.

ALBERT. She just left, my lady, with the parlour-maid.

RONA. *(after a pause)* Well, those two have agreed about something at last… We'll have the joint and the trifle.

ALBERT. Yes, my lady.

He goes back into the kitchen.

HAROLD. *(rising)* We'll give him a hand. Come on, Phyl –

PHYLLIS. I'll lay the table –

HAROLD. Get crackin' –

He and PHYLLIS *go out by the kitchen door, he closing it behind them.*

RONA. There go two that have wallowed in pitch, and feel not in the least defiled.

WILL. I used to be like that. *(sitting at the desk, and laying aside* MARIAN*'s newspaper)*

RONA. I wish in a way you still could be.

She has taken up two clipped typewritten sheets, and is looking at them.

Houses. In Guernsey?

WILL. Guernsey?

RONA. *(laying the sheets before him)* I thought it'd pull us together if we started plans. One sounds possible, I've marked it.

THANE comes in by the main door, shutting it; he looks worried.

THANE. I'm afraid there's a crowd in the road.

RONA. What are they doing?

THANE. Looking at the house. I had to stop two from climbing into the garden.

WILL. *(making to rise)* That means I've got to tell him. Now.

RONA. *(distressed, holding his arm)* Must we?

THANE. Somebody'd be bound to, even if you kept the newspapers from him.

RONA. I'll see he's kept amused for a minute.

She goes out by the main door and hurries upstairs. WILL looks down at the prospectus.

WILL. Guernsey looks pretty bleak.

THANE. Good for the creative impulse, though. Victor Hugo, and all that.

WILL. *(looking at him)* I shan't be following them.

THANE. You won't?

WILL. Once he knows, how can I ever face him again? You must see that!

THANE. *(after a pause)* Yes, I do.

WILL. No, I've got to take my punishment. Only don't tell Rona yet, she's got enough on her hands –

THANE. Where will you go?

WILL. Back to where I belong. Rotherhithe, or the equivalent. *(quickly, as RONA comes back and closes the main door)*

Don't tell her –

RONA. He's reading.

WILL. Good –

THANE. I wish I could help. *(turning to go)*

RONA. Thane – *(her voice breaking)* – I want you to reassure me – no, tell me the truth, one way or the other…

THANE. Yes, Rona?

RONA. Something Marian said – and other women will too. She suggested that Will married me because I agreed to – to tolerate. Lying awake, I've had such doubts… Thane, did I make a mistake?

WILL. What do you mean?

RONA. *(still to* **THANE***)* I wanted to marry him. Perhaps I *made* myself not mind.

If he cheated, so did I. If I'd been firm like Marian, perhaps he'd have reformed. Did I encourage him to think there was no harm? If he hadn't married, he wouldn't have accepted the knighthood anyway, and none of this would have happened. Thane…*(in tears)*… did I make a mistake?

WILL. *(standing)* Is there any reason you can't ask *me* that?

> **RONA** *does not answer, but looks at* **THANE**. **WILL** *looks away, too upset to speak.*

THANE. If Will had married a woman like Marian, she *might* have seen he didn't get into this scandal… but how do we know she'd have kept him long enough to get successful enough to *warrant* a scandal? Hard to answer… Will, two things will help you to face this. *(as* **WILL** *looks at him)* First, that we all have *one thing we're ashamed of.* All those out there have. *(designating the garden)* Even the judge has, who'll be peering at you over his glasses, making you feel like dirt. His secret may be the nastiest of the lot. Only *you* have committed the sin of being found out… The other thing is, that whatever trouble you've got into, you have *lived.* And because you've lived, you've written. Think of the master pieces round this room. If none of the men who wrote them had ever broken the law, half the books would never have seen the light of day. That's no reflection on the other half, but it's true. So in the name of… Francois Villon, Thomas de Quincey, Oscar Wilde, Baudelaire, William Shakespeare, and quite a few others… take heart. I'll never get into trouble. I don't know that I've ever lived, either.

Remember that, it'll boost your morale. *(going to the kitchen door, then turning)* If you want me, I'll be peeling potatoes.

He goes, shutting the door behind him. **RONA** *sits on the sofa, laying the newspaper on the stool.* **WILL** *crosses to her.*

WILL. You've been crying.

RONA. It's years since I cried because of you. You've a good record.

WILL. I'm glad you came out with all that, it's made me forget Ian for a minute. *(sitting next to her)* Do you remember our jokes about me never having told you I loved you? A year ago, I was hard up for something to write about. I thought, 'I'll write about my life if I'd never married Rona.' And I'm supposed to have imagination. I'd find it easier to write the life of pearl diver. Because I have no idea how I would have functioned without you.

I don't mean just the books, I mean my… too too solid flesh, that's brought us to this pass. If I hadn't married you, I would not have lived. *(as* **RONA** *turns her head and looks at him)* I trust you, and you trust me. You need me, and I need you. And you ask me if you made a mistake. Have you waited sixteen years to tell me that you can't relax until I've made you a declaration of love?

They kiss. The main door opens; it's **IAN**.

IAN. Dad, there are some people outside who look as if they want your autograph. You haven't been knighted again?

WILL. No. Opportunity knocks but once.

IAN. *(going to the window, to look)* Perhaps they just want it anyway – *(turning again)* – that wasn't from Macbeth, was it?

WILL. I don't think so.

IAN. Good–

He starts to go, then turns and looks at them, puzzled.

What are you sitting next to each other for?

RONA. Because we like each other.

IAN. Oh... Shall I bring in the autograph books?

RONA. Ian, Daddy wants to talk to you.

> IAN *comes and stands near then, inquiringly.* RONA *half rises, sees* MARIAN*'s newspaper on the stool, and places a cushion over it. She goes to the main door, where she turns.*

I'll be in the bedroom when you want me.

WILL. All right.

> RONA *goes out, closing the door.*

IAN. Yes, Dad?

WILL. Sit down, Ian, will you?

IAN. *(sitting on the sofa, next to his father)* Has something happened?

WILL. Yes.

IAN. *(worried)* Is Mummy ill?

WILL. She's all right. It's me.

IAN. *(after a pause)* Have you written yourself out?

WILL. *(smiling)* I hope not... I'm in trouble.

IAN. Trouble? Have you lost a lot of money?

WILL. Indirectly I may have, but that doesn't matter. I'm in trouble through my own fault.

IAN. Have you been speculating injudiciously?

WILL. I'm afraid, Ian, this isn't like anything in books... It'd be easier if you'd ever thought what – faults your father has, but one doesn't do that.

IAN. What faults?

WILL. Serious ones.

IAN. Oh. *(after a pause, seriously)* As bad as cruelty to animals?

WILL. *(after thought)* I don't know... But bad.

IAN. How bad?

WILL. *(slowly, with difficulty)* Ian, you remember the book of mine I found you reading, and it was too grown up for you?

IAN. *The Wanderers?* Yes.

WILL. What did you think it was about?

IAN. A house in Portsmouth.

WILL. Yes?

IAN. Some women lived in it, and some sailors came to stay.

WILL. That's right.

IAN. The women were that funny word in the Bible, weren't they – whores? *(he pronounces the 'w', as in 'which')*

WILL. That's right, whores. *(he pronounces it the same way)* They crop up in my books rather a lot.

IAN. You've come to know them, Dad, haven't you? I remember it saying that on the wireless, only in a roundabout way.

WILL. I'm afraid, Ian, I've sometimes come to know them too well.

IAN. How do you mean, Dad?

WILL. Your mother once said there was a lot of the schoolboy in me. You know how sometimes at the end of term everybody's let loose, and a sort of hysteria of high spirits breaks out, and somebody smashes a window?

IAN. A boy in my house once set fire to the dormitory.

WILL. That's what I've done.

IAN. *(incredulously)* Set fire to some women?

WILL. Set fire to something. That's what I'm realising.

IAN. You mean there was a party, and you got reckless?

WILL. *(eagerly)* That's it! You do understand what I mean?

IAN. *(warmly)* Oh yes! Was Mummy there?

A pause. **WILL** *realises that he has not progressed as far as he thought.*

WILL. No. But she knows all about it. And I'm afraid it's got into the papers.

IAN. Oh… What happened at the party?

WILL. *(after a pause)* I've got to tell you. *(slowly, with great difficulty)* People had too much to drink, and took their clothes off and fooled about, and somebody took some photographs.

IAN. *(after a pause)* You mean like smutty pictures?

WILL. Yes.

IAN. *(slowly)* Last, term, a boy had some, and he was expelled.

WILL. That's what happens.

IAN. He wasn't a very decent chap, though.

WILL. I'm not very decent either.

IAN. Did *you* take the photographs?

WILL. No no – I didn't know anything about them. But I was responsible for the party.

IAN. What made it all come to light?

WILL. There was a girl there, who looked twenty-four but turned out to be not quite fifteen.

IAN. Good Lord. *(puzzled)* A freak?

WILL. No, made up to the nines, and wearing furs and earrings. And to be responsible for a girl of her age being at that sort of party, is a serious offence.

IAN. *(after a pause)* I see.

RONA *comes in by the main door, closing it.*

WILL. I've told him.

RONA *looks fearfully at* IAN, *and comes down. He looks at her.*

IAN. *(slowly)* Isn't it a funny thing to have happened, Mummy?

RONA. Are you upset, my darling?

IAN. It's a bit sudden… *(to* WILL*)* Did you say it was in the paper?

WILL. Yes.

IAN. Can I see it?

WILL hesitates, then quickly takes the newspaper from under the cushion, and hands it to IAN, front page upwards. IAN reads. He lays aside the paper, and looks at WILL.

WILL. I'm sorry, Ian.

IAN. It says there'll be a trial. Will they send you to prison?

WILL. They may not, but they may.

IAN. *(after a pause)* If they do, it'll be in term time, so it won't seem so long…

WILL. I'm afraid, Ian, there wont be any term time, for a bit.

IAN. Why not?

WILL. It wouldn't be very pleasant for you.

IAN. *(thinking)* I suppose not. They'd pull my leg no end. Even Henderson… I rather like school.

RONA. Daddy can tutor you.

IAN. Rather fun.

RONA. *(after a look at WILL, to IAN)* Darling, are you sure you've taken all this in?

WILL. You see, I've behaved very badly –

A crash of splintering glass, as a stone comes hurtling through the window and knocks the desk lamp onto the carpet at their feet. A murmur of hostility, beyond the garden, which grows and then dies. WILL leaps to his feet, crosses, and picks up the stone and the lamp, putting the latter back on the desk. IAN has risen; RONA holds him.

IAN. *(incredulously)* It's the people outside. I thought they wanted your autograph. *(white, his eyes wide)* It's the mob, Mummy. Like the French Revolution…

RONA. Never mind, darling. We're together…

IAN. *(bewildered)* But what have we done to *them*?

RONA. Poor darling, it's so sudden –

IAN runs suddenly to WILL, flings his arms round him and bursts into tears. WILL disengages him; RONA takes him in her arms.

It's all right, my baby – it's all right –

IAN. *(through his sobs)* I was all right, till they threw that stone... What's it got to do with them... Breaking things that don't belong to them... *(gradually he quietens down)*

WILL. I'm afraid that's life, Ian.

RONA. When you're in trouble, people do those things.

IAN. *(gulping, as he recovers)* They did it to the Duke of Wellington, didn't they?

WILL. And he was old and all by himself when it happened. There are three of us.

RONA. We thought we'd take a cottage.

IAN. *(taken aback)* You mean... leave this house?

WILL. You see, it'd be difficult for Mummy, with tradespeople and so on.

IAN. Yes, I do see... I've never lived anywhere else.

RONA. I know, it's too bad. But we'll take our nice things.

IAN. *(to WILL, anxiously)* They'll let you come and live with us, won't they?

WILL. Do you think I should?

IAN. Why not?

WILL. Because I've done some very bad things.

IAN. But you can't really be as bad – as the things you've done... I don't quite know what I mean – but if you *were* bad, you wouldn't have told me the truth just now – you'd have stuffed me up with lies, wouldn't you?

RONA. That's perfectly true –

IAN. So why shouldn't you come and live with us?

WILL. Because the bad things I've done belong to my early days. And I've been feeling – *(to RONA)* – I should go back to the sort of people who belong to that time.

IAN. But that time's over. How can you still belong to it?

WILL. *(thoughtfully)* Since I met your mother, I *have* belonged less and less. But I had to be contrary.

IAN. Why?

WILL. Because I thought I had the right to be free. *(to* **RONA***)* But if you're a member of society…*(looking at the stone in his hand)*… you have to conform, or crack. You can't have it both ways.

IAN. You mean you've been contrary the way children are?

WILL. Yes. *(after a pause)* Ian d'you know what I'm doing? A bit late, but I'm doing it, with your help… I'm growing up. *(to* **RONA***)* In front of my own son. Makes you feel rather a fool.

IAN. *(to him, anxiously)* You'll stick with us?

WLLL. *(after a pause)* Yes.

> **ALBERT** *comes in from the kitchen; he sees* **IAN***, then the stone and the broken glass.*

IAN. You won't leave Albert behind?

WILL. Albert'll come.

IAN. *(after a long pause)* I think I'll go up and collect my thoughts… *(going and then turning)* The police won't be able to separate the three of us, in any way?

RONA. Cross my heart.

> **IAN** *sighs with relief, turns to go, then sees the stone in his father's hand. He goes to* **WILL***, takes the stone and hurls it back, through a pane of glass into the garden.*
>
> *A murmur from beyond the garden, faint but definite. boos and cat-calls.* **IAN** *goes out by the main door, and upstairs.*
>
> **RONA** *shuts the door after him;* **WILL** *goes to the desk, looking out of the window, and takes up the house prospectus.*

ALBERT. I thought, my lady, with the dining-room facin' the road, we'd have dinner all together down in the kitchen.

RONA. Good idea.

WILL. Like in the good old Merton Mews flat, eh, Albert?

ALBERT. *(grinning)* That's right, sir.

He hurries back into the kitchen.

WILL. *(reading from the prospectus)* 'Ridge Cottage, Red Cliff, Guernsey'. Sounds all right.

RONA. The neighbours won't be. It's very lonely.

WILL. Victor Hugo wrote reams there.

RONA. Will you get restless?

WILL. What do you think?

RONA. *(smiling)* Of course you will. You can't expect to turn into a saint overnight. I'm not sure I'd like that, anyway.

WILL. On top of the Sir, *Saint* William might be too much… Well, when I do get restless, there'll be two of you to cope.

He looks at the windows, crosses to the window, closes the curtains, and turns to go; RONA *is looking round the room.*

Beyond the garden, a swell of booing and cat-calls. WILL *stops, crosses back to the windows, and pulls the curtains violently open. He stands looking out;* RONA *walks to his side, and looks out. The noise dies away.* ALBERT *comes in from the kitchen.*

ALBERT. I fetched Ian down, sir, and it's ready when you are.

He holds the kitchen door open. RONA *turns and looks at him;* WILL *does the same.* RONA *takes* WILL*'s arm, and they move together towards the kitchen, slowly, firmly, as the curtain falls.*

ENDS

Lightning Source UK Ltd.
Milton Keynes UK
UKOW07f0500051214

242692UK00001B/5/P